Edizioni R.E.I.

Maria Papachristos

Muses - Nymphs - Other Gods

Myths and Legends of ancient Greece

Volume 3

ISBN 978-2-37297-3663

Edizioni R.E.I. France
www.edizionirei.webnode.com
edizionireifrance@outlook.com

Maria Papachristos

Muses - Nymphs

Other Gods

Edizioni R.E.I. France

Index

The Muses 9

   Clio 17

   Euterpe 19

   Talia 20

   Melpomene 21

   Tersicore 23

   Erato 24

   Polyhymnia 25

   Urania 26

   Calliope 27

The Moires or Parcae...28

The Erinni..31

The Cabiri..34

The Dactyls..35

The Curets 36

The Coribanti..37

The Gorgons 38

Pegaso...40

The Hours or Seasons 41

The Nymphs 43

   Alseadi... 48

   Oreadi 49

Napee 50

Auloniad 51

Maenads 52

Dryads 54

Hamadryads 56

Epimelidi 57

Dafnaie 58

Naiad 60

Nereids 65

Oceanine 75

Pleiades 85

Hyades 92

Eliadi 93

Hesperides 95

Night 98

Apate 100

Eris...101

Geras..103

Hypnos...103

Ker 104

Momo 104

Moros...105

Nemesis 105

Achlys...106

Thanatos 107

Oneiroi 108

Fobos 109

Lissa 109

Alfeo 110

Acheloos 111

Apeliote 112

Asclepius 113

Boreas 119

Ebe 120

Aeolus 122

Fobos 123

Iris 124

Morfeo 125

Narcissus 126

Nike 129

Pan 131

Tiche 136

Triton 138

Zefiro 139

The Muses

The Muses were the nine daughters of Zeus and Mnemosine (the "Memory") and their guide was Apollo. The importance of the muses in the Greek religion was elevated: they, in fact, represented the supreme ideal of the Art, understood as truth of the "All" that is the eternal magnificence of the divine. The Muses have a very high, indeed unique, place in the divine hierarchy. They are called daughters of Zeus, born of Mnemosyne, the Goddess of memory; but this is not all, because to them, and to them alone, it is reserved to bring, like the father himself of the Gods, the appellative of the Olympics, appellation with which they used to honor the gods in general, but, at least originally, no God in particular, made exception to Zeus and the Muses. They are the link between the immutable and capricious universe of Olympus and the restless stage of human life, as they hold the illusory key to the pursued immortality through art and knowledge.

The supreme god joined for nine nights with Mnemosine, daughter of Uranus and Gaia. At the expiration of gestation, the goddess gave birth to nine girls in the Pierìa, at the foot of Olympus. Another tradition is made by the daughters of Uranus ("the Sky") and of Gea ("the Earth"). In Homer, the Muses appear as ancient and always young goddesses of music who rejoice with their sweet song the table of the Gods of Olympus; only later did they preside over the arts, the sciences, the letters, the poetry, each with particular attributes. They were also called Heliconia, since their seat was Mount Helicon; the Elicona is made famous by Greek mythology because of two sacred springs to the Muses that are found there: Aganippe and Hippocrene, both toponyms formed on the hippo-horse root, since the tradition had it that Pegasus had gushed them. On its slopes was the village of Ascra, which gave birth to the poet Hesiod, who tells of having met the Muses while, young man, was intent on grazing the flocks on the sides of the mountain, where Eros and the Muses had already then shrines and a land for dancing near the top.

The Muses would have inspired him, and thanks to them he began to sing the origins of the gods. Thus it was that the Elicona became a symbol of poetic inspiration. In addition to the sources mentioned above, tradition has it that the source in which Narcissus mirrored himself was struck by his beauty was also found on the Elicona. Since this mountain is located in Beozia, a region inhabited by the Aoni (Aonia), they were also called Aonie. Sometimes they were also called Aganippidi, from the name of the homonymous source, Aganippe, located right near the Mount Elicona; it is said that this source had the power to change those who had watered it into poets.

The origin of the spring is attributed to a furrow in the earth made by the Pegaso hoof. In Theocritus they are called "Pierides", since a tradition placed their birth in Pieria, in Macedonia; here, in the village of Pimpleia, near Dion, the muse Calliope gave birth to Orpheus. The muses were those who had taught the famous riddle to the Sphinx, the monster generated by Echidna had by Typhon, which he proposed to the Tebans who passed through Mount Fichio.

The sphinx is a mythological figure depicted as a monster with the body of a lion and human head or hawk or goat, sometimes with wings. In Greek mythology there was a single Sphinx, a demon of destruction and bad luck. In the myth of Oedipus, the Sphinx guarded the entrance to the Greek city of Thebes.

To allow the passage to visitors, he asked them a riddle to answer correctly. Era or Ares moved the Sphinx from his homeland in Ethiopia to Thebes in Greece, where he asked all passers-by what is perhaps the most famous enigma of history: "What is that animal that walks in the morning with four paws, of day with two, and in the evening with three? " The monster strangled or devoured anyone who could not answer. In the myth, Oedipus resolved the enigma by answering: "the Man, who in childhood crawls on all fours, then walks on two feet in adulthood, and finally uses a walking stick in old age". Once the Sphinx is beaten, the story continues with the Sphinx that flows from its high rock and dies.

The enigma of the Sphinx is not a simple riddle, but a very profound question on the destiny of man. The animal that walks first with four, then with two and finally with three legs is in fact the human being, which proceeds on all fours a few months from birth, then on the legs in the arc of life, and finally, in old age leaning on the stick to support yourself. The Sphinx, in an enigmatic form, interrogates man on himself, on the fragility of his existence, as well as on the brevity of this, imagining human life in the subtle space of a day. This mythical episode highlights the symbolic characteristics of the Sphinx. Here existential questioning and fascination with power are linked in one of the most famous and meaningful events of the Greek myth. Oedipus, raised without knowing it by adoptive parents, learns from an oracle who will have to kill his father and join his mother. Upset, he immediately leaves his home, and sets off for Thebes. On the street he meets, without knowing who he is, the king of the city, Laius, and for a futile reason he kills him. Thebes, left without sovereign, decides to entrust the throne to those who will solve the enigma of the Sphinx, which terrorizes precisely the Theban region. Oedipus, undefeated in the prodigious being, is able to give an answer to the enigma.

The power over the city is therefore his. He enters triumph in Thebes and marries Laio's wife, Giocasta, from whom he has four children. One day, however, a terrible pestilence breaks out in the city, and the oracle forces to expel the one who defiles, with his impiety, all the Theban people. Oedipus sets off in search of the guilty and discovers the terrible truth: not only the person responsible for the death of the previous sovereign is himself, but Laius and Jocasta are, in reality, his real parents.

Thus the prophecy is fulfilled on its terrible fate: to kill one's father and to unite with his mother. The Sphinx tested the man, who, trusting on his own strength, gained power and believed he could lead his life. But in Greek religiosity one can not go beyond the limits imposed on man by fate: so Oedipus loses power and fulfills his tragic destiny. Apollo was the protector of the Muses, so they were invited to the parties of the gods and heroes to cheer the guests with songs and dances, often singing together. They often cheered Zeus, their father, singing the exploits.

The Muses were also considered the depositories of memory (Mnemosine was the goddess of memory and knowledge) as daughters of Zeus. Their cult was widespread among the

Pythagoreans. Their earliest song was that aimed at the victory of the Gods against the Titans' revolt.

They cheered each party with their song, remembered them in the case of the wedding of Cadmus and Harmony and Thetis and Peleus, while complaining about the loss of the brave Achilles for seventeen days and seventeen nights.

The Muses were "in charge of Art in every field", anyone who dared to challenge them was severely punished: the sirens were deprived of their wings, then used by the same Muse to make them crowns. The Pierides, nine like the muses, challenged them to the song, asking in case of victory the sacred sources to the adversaries; after the trial of the Pierids it was Calliope who participated in the muses and after a long song won and the women were turned into birds.

Their magnificence enchanted Pyrenees, who, after conquering Daulis and part of Phocis, died in their pursuit. It was Apollo who convinced them to abandon their ancient home, Mount Helicon, taking them to Delphi. The Muses do not possess a legendary cycle of their own, each of them is given some love adventure. Calliope is the mother of Orpheus, the most famous poet and musician ever.

Apollo gave him the lira and the Muses taught him to use it. Urania or Terpsichore is considered the mother of Lino, who was a remarkable musician, who dared to rival Apollo himself and he, indignant, killed him. Aristeus, son of Apollo and the nymph Cyrene, was taken care of by the muses that offered him in the bride Autonoe, from which he had two sons, Actaeon and Macride. The muses were kind to him, they taught him the principles of the medical arts, of healing and the ability to make prophecies, in exchange Aristeo looked after their flocks that he was grazing in the plains of Ftia. He fell in love with Eurydice, then he married Orpheus. When the brave Orfeo, son of one of the muses, Calliope, and of the sovereign Thracian Eagro, was torn to pieces and thrown into the sea, they were to collect the scattered limbs and decided to bury him in Libetra, near the slopes of Mount Olympus. He was the son of one of the nine Muses (Clio, Calliope, Euterpe or Tersicore) also Reso, the young and beautiful king of Thrace, who was brought up by some Naiads (nymphs who presided over all the sweet waters of the earth and possessed healing faculties). prophetic). Reso went up again adolescent on the throne of Thrace, succeeding the father who had abdicated in his favor.

He had recently become king when the news of the war broke out between Greeks and Trojans, and then sent to the help of King Priam a large contingent of men led by two mature nobles, Acamante (uncle of Cizico, the late sovereign of the Dolioni) and Piroo: if he could not immediately intervene directly in the first person it was because at the same time he found himself having to defend his kingdom from an attack by the inhabitants of Scythia. Ten years passed, and finally Reso arrived in Troia with two white horses that had been donated by Ares, with a great speed. The Achaeans, worried about this, sent Ulysses and Diomedes to steal them. The two heroes, entered the camp with the favor of darkness, entered the tent of Reso: Diomede with the sword hit the king's throat and twelve of his men while they slept, then move away with the precious animals stolen in the meantime from Ulysses. Ironically, the young leader was dreaming of being killed by Diomedes, which had contributed to further agitating his sleep, since he was already a great snorer in itself. Ippocoon, cousin and age of Reso, and his advisor survived the massacre. In the tragedy Reso, whose attribution to Euripides is still uncertain and contested, it is said that the young lord of the Thracians was killed the very night of his arrival in Troy without having had time to quench the horses with the Scamander's water , in which case the city would become impregnable. Exhausted by the hardships of the journey, he set out to sleep in his bed. In this work is also celebrated the extraordinary beauty of the hero, defined as "similar to a nume" while he incurs on his beautiful combat chariot. In the end of the tragedy, the Muse mother of Reso (she never makes the name of it) takes with her the corpse of the hero, and though torn by her premature death reveals that he will be resurrected by the gods of the underworld; after his body and soul are reunited, Reso will even obtain immortality. However, it will have to remain in the bowels of the earth, far away from men but also from the kingdom of the dead. Of the place that will welcome the hero in his new status of being immortal it is said only that it is inaccessible to all, including deities, and that its darkness is inferior to that of Hades, a place of great beauty, though not as luminous as the Elysian Fields, which should give Reso a sense of happiness despite the forced isolation. The most important and the most splendid of all the sanctuaries dedicated to the Muses in Greece was that of the Elicona, in which every five years great feasts were celebrated that included mainly musical and poetic competitions; later they were enriched with tragedies, comedies, satiresque dramas. They were celebrated until the time of Constantine. With Greek literature the Muses also entered Rome, and according to the tradition, Numa Pompilius first consecrated them an aedicule on the Celio and a grove irrigated by sources, especially by the famous source of the nymph Egeria. Poor was their importance in worship. A single temple was raised by Fulvio Nobiliore, where they were associated with Hercules, and only helped to make them more popular with the Camens, indigenous deities of the prophetic inspiration, which occurred when Fulvio dedicated his temple. According to the order made by Hesiod, the names of the Muses were:

- Clio – the History, the one who makes famous, depicted with a scroll in his hand. Clio, the elder sister, the first among the muses, receives from the mother Mnemosine, personification of memory, the power to transmit the memory of facts and characters.
- Euterpe - the Music, the one who rejoices, depicted with a flute better called "Aulos". The ancient Greek Aulos, often erroneously translated as "flute", was a cane (reed) instrument with two reeds, like the oboe and, according to the legend, it was invented by Euterpe himself.
- Talia - the Comedy, the one that is festive, depicted with a mask, an ivy garland and a stick. It is considered the mother with Apollo of the Coribanti who, in Greek mythology, are priests of the goddess Cybele, who invented the frame drum and with it created a music based on the obsessive rhythm that was used to treat epilepsy and to defeat the melancholy of Jupiter.
- Melpomene - the Tragedy, the one who sings, depicted with a mask, a sword and the stick of Hercules.

Melpomene would be, according to some, the mother of the sirens fabulous beings represented with head of woman and body of bird, (according to other versions with body of fish), whose seductive voice attracted the sailors to make them die.

- Terpsichore - the Dance, the one who delights in the dance, depicted with a plectrum and lyre and crowned with laurel, the plant sacred to Apollo.
- Erato – the lyric and anacreontic poetry, derives its name from Eros (love). She is represented as a nymph crowned with myrtles and roses, holding a lyre in her left hand and an arch in her right hand.
- Polymnia - the Mime, the one who has many hymns. Polimnia is attributed to the inventions of the lira and agriculture. It is depicted with a crown of flowers or pearls, dressed white, the right hand in the act of haranguing and in the left a scepter.
- Urania – the Astronomy, she who is celestial, depicted dressed in a blue dress, crowned with stars, with a stick, or forefinger, pointing at the sky. According to Hesiod it was loved by Apollo, giving birth to Lino and Orpheus, mythical singers. According to Catullus, it was the mother of Hymen, the god of marriage, whose father was Bacchus.
- Calliope - the epic poetry, the one who has a beautiful voice, depicted with a tablet covered with wax and a stylus, with a crown of gold at the head. Epic poetry is the versed tale of the legendary exploits of a people, its myths and its heroes. The "moral" task of epic poetry was to exalt the values of friendship, courage, love, family, gratitude and peace.

Those who dared to offend the Muses were severely punished, like the Pierides, nine sisters daughters of Pierio, king of Thessaly, and of Evippa. Their names were:
- Colimba
- Iunce
- Cencride

- Cissa
- Chloride
- Acalantide
- Nessa
- Pipo
- Dracontide

Skilled in singing, they went to Mount Helicon, the seat of the Muses to challenge them in a singing contest; Calliope also sang for the sisters and the Nymphs, nominated referees of the contest, declared the Muses victorious. Le Pieridi, instead of humbly accepting the defeat, began to insult the Nymphs, so that the Muses, to punish them, turned them into birds (colimbo, torticollis, cencride, jay, greenfin, goldfinch, duck, woodpecker and draconte), according to Ovid in piche (magpies). Even Tamiri, a young man of rare beauty, dared to challenge them. The Tamiri singer from Ecalia boasted of his singing skills and challenged the Muses to Dorio, proposing, in case of victory, to join after all, while if he had lost, they would have been able to dispose of his body. When the race ended with the defeat of Tamiri, the goddesses, irritated, blinded him and deprived him of his musical ability. During the Middle Ages, an allegorical interpretation was shown by the mythographer Fulgenzio, according to whom the Muses would represent nine progressive moments of the doctrinal activity:

- Clio, the first approach to science by desire for glory.
- Euterpe, the confirmation in this approach for the pleasure that derives from it.
- Melpomene, meditation, or study.
- Talia, the receptive capacity.
- Polimnia, the memory.
- Erato, the inventive effort.
- Tersicore, discriminating judgment.
- Urania, the proper discernment of a celestial mind.
- Calliope, the catchy expression.

Clio

Depicted sitting and with a parchment in hand, Clio represented History. Clio, the elder sister, the first among the muses, receives from the mother Mnemosine, personification of memory, the power to transmit the memory of facts and characters.

Clio, "She who can make famous" is therefore Muse of history. In ancient times this Muse was invoked by the poets who were about to compose texts that would have contained historical facts such as Stazio who, in Thebaide, invokes her as the inspirer of his poem. According to one version, he had the son Reso by king Strimone, who later became a river god. It is represented with a trumpet in the right hand and a parchment on the left. The myth tells that after an altercation with Aphrodite, the latter punished her by making her fall in love with Pierio (king of Macedonia). From their union they would descend Giacinto, Imene and Ialemo.

In the literary myth Giaconto represents a young man of exceptional beauty, loved by the god Apollo, but much admired and desired also by Zephyr, the west wind. Apollo's love for him was so great that, in spite of being constantly close to the boy, he neglected all his principal activities and accompanied his inseparable lover wherever he went. One day the two began a competition to launch the disc; Apollo launched first, but the disk, diverted in its trajectory by a gust of wind raised by the jealous Zephyr, ended by striking at the temple Giacinto, thus wounding him to death. Apollo tried to save the beloved teenager by using every medical art he knew, but he could do nothing against destiny. He decided, at that point, to turn the handsome boy into a flower with an intense color, the same one of the blood that Giacinto had poured from the wound.

Before returning to Heaven, the god, bent over the newly created flower, wrote his syllables "ai", "ai" with his own fist on the petals, as an undying monument of sorrow tried for such misfortune, which had deprived him of love and of love. friendship of the young. This expression of pain, still today, is to be seen in the signs that seem to be engraved on the leaves of the Hyacinth and which are similar to the letters A and I (sign of the divine laments for the loss suffered). According to Ovid, it was instead the divine tears that colored the petals of the newly created flower, thus giving it the imperishable sign of the pain experienced; this mythological flower has been identified over time with various different plants, including the Iris, the Delphinium and the violet of thought: other dead semidivine figures in the flower of their youth have also been transformed into "protectors of vegetative life", for example Narcissus, Ciparisso and Adonis himself. Apollodorus says that Tamiri was also known to have been one of the previous lovers of Giacinto, therefore also the first human being to have loved another male and thus giving rise to pederasty. Clio, muse of the story, was immortalized in 1632 by the artist Artemisia Gentileschi with a painting, preserved in the collections of the Pisan museum, which touches the effects of energetic and throbbing photographic power. Far from any stereotyped canon and far from the most familiar narrative-inspired inspiration, the Clio muse of Gentileschi is animated by the fascination that human events and the characters who were artisans lit in the refined sensibility of the Roman painter.

The figure shown here, wearing luxurious clothes, occupies the space with classical and thoughtful composure, has the hand resting on the side and with bold and regal, wearing the laurel wreath, symbol of immortality, and the trumpet, symbol of the Fama. The painting was designed to commemorate the figure of François Rosières, advisor to the powerful Giuse family.

Euterpe

Became the Muse of music and lyric poetry and according to some inventors of the aulos, although most of the scholars of mythology has granted this honor to the satyr Marsyas, as we read in the myth of Marsyas and Apollo. Aulos was an air-conditioned musical instrument used in Ancient Greece.

It consisted of a cane tube, made of wood, or of bone or ivory, with a bulb-shaped mouthpiece and its reed. It is often seen as depicted in the form of two divergent tubes, in which case it is called diaulos. Sometimes the Greek word aulos is erroneously translated into Italian with flute, a generic name for cutting sound aerophones. In reality, the aulos, a double-reed instrument, belongs to the oboe family.

It is believed to have been played with the circular breathing technique. In the classical era, up to five holes were made on the pipes; in the Hellenistic-Roman age a greater number.

Talia

Muse of comedy, presided over the comedy, playful poetry and idyll and was represented with a comic mask in one hand and in the other a shepherd's stick, on the head had a crown of ivy.

It is considered the mother with Apollo of the Coribanti who, in Greek mythology, are priests of the goddess Cybele, who invented the frame drum and with it created a music based on the obsessive rhythm that was used to treat epilepsy and to defeat the melancholy of Jupiter.

The frame drum is a percussion musical instrument consisting of a single skin mounted on a ring with small metal cymbals, or without the latter case in which it is sometimes referred to as "mute".

Technically a framed drum is defined as a drum whose depth is less than the diameter.

Melpomene

Muse of the song in general, then of the tragedy, he wore a tragic mask, the club of Hercules and a sword, his head was crowned with vine leaves and he wore the coturni, an ancient shoe, similar to an ankle boot made of strips of leather or other intertwined, traditional tragic sandals. Melpomene is depicted richly dressed, with a severe and severe look; with this, the muse indicates that tragedy is a very difficult art that requires exceptional ingenuity and a vigorous imagination. Tragedy is one of the oldest forms of theater.

Its origins are obscure, but they certainly derive from the rich poetic and religious tradition of ancient Greece. The tragedy was born around the sixth century BC in Ancient Greece, in honor of the god Dionysus, who was celebrated with dances, songs and parties. The origin of the term is shrouded in mystery: according to the most accredited theories the first part of the name should be put in relation with "tràgos" "goat" and the second with "oidè" "canto"; in fact it is thought that the tragedy is probably so called or because the winner of the contest obtained, in fact, a goat as a reward (song for the goat), or because the coreuti wore masks with goat-like masks (capri singing). Aristotle states that the tragedy comes from the satirical Drama. Moreover, in the Poetics (1450), he defines tragedy as an imitation of a serious and accomplished action in itself, which has a certain width, a language decorated in different proportions according to the different parts, is carried out by means of characters who act on the scene and do not narrate. In ancient times Athens claimed the paternity of the tragedy, even if the language in which the Chorus expressed itself is the Doric language.

According to some traditions, from the union of Melpomene with the river god Acheloo (son of Oceano and Teti) would be born the Sirens, fabulous beings represented with head of woman and body of bird, (according to other versions with body of fish), whose seductive voice attracted the sailors and then

lead them to certain death. Other sources tell us in Melpomene
the mother of the musician Tamiri.

Tersicore

Muse of dance and choral poetry, he was holding a lyre and a plectrum and a garland of flowers on his head.
Usually it is depicted with clothes similar to those of the aedi and crowned with laurel leaves always intent to draw agreements with the tapered fingers in his instrument.
From Tersicore comes the word "tersicoreo" which means linked to dance. Here it is interpreted with an unusual iconography, like Musa of lyric poetry.
Started by Canova as a portrait of Alexandrina Bleschamps, wife of Lucien Bonaparte, it was finished as it now appears on behalf of Count Sommariva, who took over the commission and made Canova change the head depicting Bleschamps with the current one, idealized and without a model specific.
There is an autograph copy of the work in the Cleveland Muscum of Art

Erato

Depicted as a young nymph crowned with myrtles and roses, holding a lyre in her left hand and holding a plectrum in the other. Often, placed near her, there is a Amorino armed with bow and quiver (quiver).

Erato, which is said to mean "Amabile", derives the name from Eros and is considered the inspirer of lyric poetry, of choral singing and of anacreontic poetry, poetry that rejects heroic values in exchange for a new equilibrium, situated in the chant , in love, in temperance that favors peace.

Erato is the muse connected to love and many ancient poets invoke her in the amorous compositions.

Tamiri was born to her (a lyre player, then a poet and a singer) and Cleomene (who later became a spouse of Flegias). Also from his union with Arcade was born Azano.

Polyhymnia

Polyhymnia presides over the orchestral, the pantomime, the dance associated with the sacred and heroic song. Sometimes it is also associated with rhetoric, memory, geometry and history. The typical iconography sees her represented as a devout looking young woman, wrapped in veil and cloak, with her head surrounded by a crown of pearls. The invention of the lyre and of agriculture is also attributed to Polyhymnia. An isolated tradition makes it the mother of Orpheus, whom she would have had from Eagro (more generally the mother of Orpheus is Calliope). Plato cites a legend that considers Polinnia mother of Eros. The invention of the lyre and of agriculture is also attributed to Polyhymnia.

The Musa Polyhymnia, a true masterpiece of ancient sculpture, embellished the imperial residence of the Horti Liciniani, a splendid villa that literary sources attribute to Emperor Licinius Gallienus and which continued to live even after the death of the emperor. The Muse was found hidden in an underground gallery to subtract it, perhaps, from the danger of barbarian invasions.

Urania

He was the muse of astronomy and geometry.

She is shown dressed in a blue dress, crowned with stars, while holding with her hands a globe that seems to measure or having always near a globe placed on a tripod and various mathematical instruments. In his hands, Urania almost always kept a compass, as evidence of the close ties that existed for astronomers between astronomy, geometry and mathematics. Many Greek mythographers attributed to the divine Urania a son, Lino, whom the muse would have generated with the god Apollo or with the theban Anfimaro.

A singer of considerable talent, Lino had perfected the sound of the lyre by replacing the gut strings with those of vegetable fiber. Among his merits, moreover, was the invention of the rhythm and perhaps of the melody, as well as the diffusion in Greece of the Phoenician alphabet, which some believe was taught by the Theban hero Cadmus. All too aware of his qualities, Lino nevertheless finished his head, committing a fatal error: he challenged the art of singing Apollo, who, annoyed by such arrogance, killed him.

Another version of the myth claimed instead that to kill Lino was Heracles, exasperated by the continuous punishment of that teacher too strict towards his poor musical attitude. According to Catullus, it was the mother of Hymen, the god of marriage, whose father was Bacchus.

Calliope

From the beautiful voice, Muse of poetry in general, then epic poetry, is represented with a roll of paper or a box of books and a stylus. Epic poetry is the versed tale of the legendary exploits of a people, its myths and its heroes. Known as the Muse of Homer, the inspirer of the Iliad and the Odyssey.
The "moral" task of Epic Poetry was to exalt the values of friendship, courage, love, family, gratitude and peace. He had two sons, Orpheus and Lino whose father according to the legends was Apollo or the king of Thrace Eagro. She was loved by her father Zeus, and he generated the Coribanti from him. She was the greatest and wisest of the Muses, as well as the most self-confident. He was the judge in the dispute over Adonis between Aphrodite and Persephone, deciding that each one would spend the same amount of time with him. She was also an inspirer of Dante in the Divine Comedy, which invokes her in the second canto of Hell and in I canto del Purgatorio.

The Moires or Parcae

The three Moires, similar to the Roman Parcae, appear twice in Hesiod's Theogony: as daughters of the Night and as daughters of Zeus and Themes, they were the personification of the ineluctable destiny. Their task was to weave the thread of every man's fate, to carry it out and finally to cut it and mark its death. The Moires were three:

- Cloto - She was the youngest and traditionally associated with birth. It was the weaver, who was spinning the stamen of life.
- Lachesis - It was the moira that held the stamen of life on the spindle, distributed the amount of life to every human and decided fate.
- Atropos - The eldest of the three sisters is the one who can not be avoided, the inflexible; it represents the final destiny of the death of each individual because she was assigned the task of cutting, with shining shears, the thread that represented the life of the individual, decreeing the moment of death. Eaco is the judge who controls in Tartarus if people enter against the will of Atropos.

The length of the threads produced can vary, exactly like that of men's life. A very short life will correspond to a very short life, like that of a newborn, and vice versa. For example, it was thought that Sophocles, one of the most long-lived Greek authors (90 years), had had a very long thread.

These are three women with an elderly appearance who live in the realm of the dead, Hades. The sensible detachment perceived by these figures and their total indifference to the life of men accentuate and perfectly represent the fatalistic mentality of the ancient Greeks. Pindar, in later times, indicated her as the servants of Temi, at her marriage to Zeus. They often acted against the will of Zeus. But all the gods were bound to obey them, for their existence guaranteed the order of the universe, to which even the gods were subject. Although many think that the

Moires had only one eye and that if they passed each other, we must say that it is a mistaken belief.

This characteristic, in fact, is proper to Graes, as can be clearly seen in the myth of Perseus, where the latter are described with only one eye and one tooth, of which they use in turn. And it is precisely this weakness that will allow Perseus to discover the Gorgon hiding place. The Graes, also known as Forcidi in Greek mythology, were daughters of Forco and Ceto. Born old, they were sisters and custodians of the Gorgons and lived in the extreme West, on the threshold of the village of the night, where the Sun never shines, in a cave on the side of the mountain of Atlas. According to the poet Hesiod, they were called Enio, Penfredo and Deino.

They embodied and symbolized the various moments of old age: in fact, they had never experienced youth and had only one eye and one tooth in common. They guarded access to the place where their sisters lived, the Gorgons. When Perseus was hunting Medusa, he stole their one eye and forced them to confess where their helmets, knapsacks and sandals were, indispensable objects to kill Medusa. The fact that the Graes had only one eye in common, allowed Perseus to pass without being seen, and immediately afterwards, he met the goddess Athena, who gave him a shining and polished shield, so that he could see the reflection of Medusa without fixing it in the eyes. The Moires never had an exact limitation: now they appear subjected to Zeus, now they are an uncontrollable, dark force, which overpowers all the gods, not except Zeus.

Zeus weighs the lives of men and informs the Moire of his decisions, can, they say, change his mind and intervene in favor of those who want, even if the thread of life of him, spun from the spindle of Cloto and measured by Lachesi, is about to be severed by Atropos's scissors. On the contrary, men even claim to be able to save themselves, within certain limits, by changing their destiny thanks to prudence in avoiding useless risks. The younger gods then laugh at the Moire and some say that Apollo one day managed to drunk them with a scam to save the life of his friend Admetus.

Others believe instead that Zeus himself must submit to the Moires, as the Pythaper priestess once said in an oracle; in fact the Moires are not daughters of Zeus, but they were born for parthenogenesis by the Great Goddess Necessity, with which the Gods do not dare to contend, and which is called "The Mighty Moire". It is generally believed that the Moires were not able to determine fate, yet in the myth of Meleager they play a decisive role. In fact, when the boy turned seven, Le Moire appeared in the room of Altea and announced that the son could live only until a certain brand of fire had been consumed. Altea immediately removed the ember from the fire, extinguished it in a bucket of water and hid it in a bonnet. But the day when Meleager killed his uncles, brothers of the mother Altea, this, saddened, threw a curse against Meleager. The Moires advised her to take the ember off the bonnet and throw it on the fire, and Meleager breathed out. In mythology the Moire do not appear that rarely.

They fought alongside Zeus in the battle against the Giants and with fiery bullets burned the heads of Agrio and Toante, and then at the battle against Typhon, always to help Zeus, they offered the monster ephemeral fruits making him believe that they would give him strength, while instead predestined to sure death.

The Moires assigned to Aphrodite only one divine task, that of making love; but one day Athena surprised her while secretly weaving to a loom, and complained that she tried to usurp her prerogatives; Aphrodite made her an apology and since then she has not even raised a finger to work.

Poets normally represent them as old and deformed women; figurative art as severe youths, characterized by Cloth with the spindle, Lachesis with a globe on which he indicates the destinies, Atropos with a scale and with the scissors with which to cut off the stamen of life. In Delphi only two Moirs are honored, those of the Birth and Death, and in Athens, Aphrodite Urania is said to be the greater of the three.

The Erinni

The Erinni are, in religion and in Greek mythology, the feminine personifications of revenge (Furies in Roman mythology) especially against those who strike relatives or members of their clan. According to the myth they were born from the blood of Uranus, who escaped when Cronus evaded him, while the subsequent poetic tradition tells them daughters of the Night.

The Erinni are three sisters:

- Aletto - the incessant - According to some Aletto was born from Acheron and from the Night (or from Gea, the Earth, according to others), its name does not have a unique etymology today. It probably means "she who does not rest", "she who does not give rest," but some interpreters are inclined towards "the unspeakable", "the one whose name can not be pronounced".
- Megera - the envious - She was in charge of envy and jealousy and induced to commit crimes, like matrimonial infidelity.
- Tisiphon - the avenger - Was charged with punishing murders of murder: patricide, fratricide, matricide, murder. A myth tells that he fell in love with the handsome Citerone hero, but he despised his love. Then Tisiphon turned one of his hair into a snake that killed Citerone with a bite. His name was given to the mountain which, before, was called Asterione.

In order to appease them, they were also called Eumenides (that is, the "benevolent"), offered various offers to them and the black sheep were sacrificed to them. The Erinni were also indicated with other epithets, such as Semnai or Potnie ("venerable"), Manie ("crazy") and Ablabie ("without fault"). They were represented as winged genes, with their mouths wide open in the act of hunting terrible screams, with snakes instead of hair, bearing torches or whips or coals and burning embers in their hands.

Their appearance was therefore of three winged women with hair of snakes that they carried in the hands of the weapons that they used to torture the unfortunate. Their task was to avenge the crimes, especially those committed against their family, torturing the murderer with the weapons they carried with them, until it went crazy.

According to some authors, the Erinni lived in Tartarus and when they did not cross the earth to punish the guilty, they dedicated themselves to torturing the damned. This double dwelling is perhaps connected to the two different stories of their birth: daughters of the Earth or Night, but according to an alternative version they were born of Hades, god of Tartarus and Persephone, and just as the two gods of the underworld had a double nature , benign and malignant. Often present in classical culture they often returned, as a cultured reference, both in medieval culture - Dante indicates it as the guardians of the infernal city of Dite - as in modern and contemporary, even if, in the latter, quite sporadically.

They are also found in the novel "Le Benevole" by Jonathan Littell and in the novel "Fury" by Salman Rushdie. Also mentioned by Marcel Proust in "In the shadow of the girls in bloom". The Erinni persecuted Alcmeone after the murder of his mother and tormented Pentesilea who had inadvertently killed his sister on a hunting trip. Alcmeone was one of the Epigones who led the second expedition against the city of Thebes. After the victory, he returned to Argos and killed his mother Erifle, who had convinced Anfiarao to participate in the expedition in which he found his death, with the sole purpose of taking possession of the necklace of the eternal youth of Harmony, kept in the coffers of Thebes.

Erifle, however, before dying, launched anathema against his son, who was pursued relentlessly for many days by the fury of the Erinni, going mad. Alcmeone then arrived at the court of Tegeo, king of Psofi in Arcadia, who convinced the god Apollo to erase the curse. He succeeded, and was able to marry Alfesibea, daughter of Tegeo. When the hero of Argo decided to donate the necklace of Harmony to his wife, the Erinni reappeared, unleashing a tremendous famine in Arcadia.

Alcmeone was therefore forced to leave again and reached the mouth of the Acheloo river.

Here he settled on a new island, formed after a flood. Following the advice of an oracle, he went in search of the god of the river Acheloo, as his purification could stop the fury of the Erinni.

Once he achieved his goal, he married Calliroe, daughter of Achelous, who gave him two sons: Acarnanus and Anfotero. Calliroe, however, when she learned of the necklace, pretended that her husband would give it to him, forcing him to return to Psofi.

Alcmeone managed to get it back, promising that he would offer it to the sanctuary of Apollo on the island of Delphi, but when the king of Psofi knew his true intentions, he had him killed by his sons. Alfesibea, to avenge the death of his beloved, agreed with Calliroe and the children that he had generated with Alcmeone: he attracted in an isolated place the brothers, who here found the death at the hands of the sons of Alcmeone. In the Medea of Euripides the chorus invokes the divine ray to stop, to avoid the impending double infanticide, the hand of Medea, possessed by the sanguinary Erinni, who instills in it the spirit of revenge.

The Cabiri

The Cabiri were a group of enigmatic gods from the underworld. They were venerated as Great Gods in a mystery cult that had its center on the island of Samothrace, in the Sanctuary of the Great Gods, and was closely linked to that of Hephaestus. Here it is said that the god of genius Hephaestus fell in love with Caberio, daughter of Proteus, and made her his lover.

From this union was born a son, that Cadmino, who in turn he had three sons, the Cabiri, and three daughters, the Cabridi.

According to Pausanias, in the place where Kabirion was contemporary to him there existed a city and men called Kabeiroi. Demeter went to one of them called Prometheus and gave them something to keep, called teletext.

At the time of the Epigoni the Cabiri were driven from their homes by the Argives. The cult spread rapidly throughout the Greek world during the Hellenistic period, and was later also adopted by the Romans. Originally, the cabiri were probably fertility deities from Frigia, protectors of the sailors, who were acquired in the Greek pantheon.

According to other studies, the Cabiri were really sons of Hephaestus, goldsmiths and fire teachers. His father's helpers in the manufacture of weapons and jewels. The origin remains unknown. The name of Cadmilo is often confused with that of Hermes, the messenger god.

Even the term Cabiri is sometimes confused with that of other groups, as in the case of Dattili, Cureti or Coribanti.

The Dactyls

In Greek mythology, some sons of Rea are called Dattili. According to some, as she was giving birth to Zeus, Rhea, gripped by her pain, moved her fingers to the ground, crushing them with such force that the Dactyls came out, five males from the right hand and five females from the other hand. Some say they lived on Mount Ida long before the birth of Zeus. Others that the nymph Anchiale gave them to life in the cave of the Ditte.

The dactyl brothers were very good blacksmiths; in fact, they were the first to discover the iron, in a nearby mountain, the Berecinzio. Instead their sisters established in Samothrace, had mastery in the art of magic and began Orpheus to the mystery of the goddess. The names are kept in secret.

Others argue instead that the Dactylians were the Curets who defended the god Zeus, when at an early age was in Crete and to escape the fury of Kronos immediately erected a temple to him. Their names were:

- Heracles
- Peonio
- Epimede
- Giasio
- Acesida
- Acmone
- Damnameneo
- Celmi

The Curets

The Curets were a group of minor deities of the Greek religion, part of the courtship of Rhea, wife of Cronus.

They were repeatedly identified with the Coribanti.

Referred to as a people of Etolia in the ninth book of the Iliad of Homer, they are more often connected to the myth of the birth of Zeus: the mother Rea, when giving birth, for fear that even the last of her children could be swallowed by Chrono, he fled to Crete; here he found the Curetes, driven from their land, the Euboea, from his father and landed on this island with his mother Chalcis.

When Rhea gives birth to Zeus, they are ready to protect the child from the familiality of Kronos.

Their dances and the noise of the weapons beaten against the shields manage to hide the little Zeus's wails.

The Coribanti

The Coribanti were the priests of Cybele, a deity born from the union between Gaia and Uranus. Different and contrasting are the traditions related to their origins: the six most likely and accepted versions are:

- Sons of Saoco and of the nymph Combe.
- Children of Cronus.
- Sons of Helios and Athena.
- Children of Zeus and of the Calliope muse.
- Sons of Apollo and of the muse Talia.
- Alternatively, sons of Apollo and of the nymph Retia.

Their number varied: three, or nine or ten, with the characteristic oscillation of all these collectivities.

Ignored by Homer and Hesiod, they were considered inventors of orgiastic dances, with frenetic music of wind instruments and timpani. This choreutical-musical orgy was attributed purifying and healing action. The ritual consisted first of a search aimed at identifying the divinity from which the subject was possessed, proposing different musical stimuli, each belonging to a precise divinity; the subject reacted only to that pertinent to the divinity that possessed him, that therefore could be appeased with the sacrifices. Then a dance took place in which the exorcized participated. This choreutic-musical therapeutic technique is very precise in the ethnological world gravitating more or less on the Mediterranean (ceremonial tsar and bori in North Africa) and, in folklore, as it remains of tarantism in southern Italy and similar practices (argia in Sardinia). According to the legend they honored their divinity with wild and orgiastic dances, during which wounds were often inflicted.

Inventors of the frame drum, created music based on the obsessive rhythm to cure epilepsy and to defeat the melancholy of Zeus. They also honored the pine in honor of Attis (son of the goddess). They were often identified with the Curetes and the Great Gods of Samothrace.

The Gorgons

The Gorgons are monsters of the Greek mythology daughters of Forco and Ceto. They were three sisters:

- Steno
- Eurial
- Medusa

Monstrous in appearance, they had golden wings, hands with bronze claws, boar's fangs and snakes instead of hair, and anyone looking at them directly in the eyes remained petrified. The gorgon par excellence was Medusa, the only mortal of the three and their queen, who, at the behest of Persephone, was the guardian of the Underworld. The Gorgons represented perversion in its three forms:

- Euriale represented sexual perversion.
- Steno, moral perversion. Steno and Euriale, unlike Medusa, were immortal (but for Virgil, all three sisters were mortal). The mythographers are in disagreement in indicating the place where he lived, according to Hesiod was near the garden of the Hesperides, while Herodotus supposes that he lived in Libya.
- Medusa, intellectual perversion. According to some authors (Ovid, Apollodorus, Hesiod) Medusa was originally a beautiful woman: to change her into a monster would have been the goddess Athena, as a punishment for having lain with Poseidon in one of his temples; according to other versions still, Athena was adverse to Medusa because the latter had dared to compete with her in beauty. Some authors have attempted to rationalize the myth of Medusa. Pausanias, for example, in the Greek period of Greece, affirms that Medusa would have been the queen of the populations living around Lake Tritone, succeeded by her father Forco after their death; to their guide he went hunting and in battle. On one of these occasions, while she was

encamped against Perseus's troops, she would be murdered at night. Perseus, admiring its beauty, would have brought his head with him to show it to the Greeks. Diodorus Siculus also tries a rational explanation, stating that the Gorgons were actually members of a race of female warriors living in Libya, against whom Perseus went to war.

The myth tells that Perseus, having received the order to deliver the head of Medusa to Polidette, lord of the island of Serifo, first went to the Graie, sisters of the Gorgons, forcing them to show him the way to reach the Nymphs.

From these he received winged sandals, a saddlebag and a helmet that made invisible: gifts to which a mirror was added by Athena and a sickle by Hermes. So armed, Perseus flew against the Gorgons and, while they were asleep, looking at the image in the divine mirror of Athena to avoid being petrified, he cut off the head to Medusa and immediately closed it in the Graie's bag. The winged horse Pegasus and Crisaore, father of Gerion, emerged from the decapitated trunk of Medusa, along with the streams of blood.

Perseus donated the head of the gorgon to the goddess Athena, who stared at her in the middle of her shield to terrorize her enemies. Even the blood of the Gorgon was endowed with magical powers: the one gushed from the left vein was a deadly poison, while that of the right vein resurrected the dead and was used by Asclepius, son of Apollo, who practiced the art of medicine. His only curl ensured victory over his adversaries, and Heracles gave one to Cepheus, as a gift from Athena, to obtain his covenant and his twenty sons in an expedition against Sparta. He told him that he could leave quietly and leave his city unattended, as long as his daughter waved Medusa's curl above the walls against the enemies who had attacked her.

Pegaso

Pegasus is a figure in Greek mythology, the most famous of winged horses. According to the myth, it was born from the ground wet with the blood shed when Perseus cut off Medusa's neck.
According to another version, Pegasus would have jumped straight out of the monster's cut neck, along with Crisaore.
A wild and free animal, Pegaso is initially used by Zeus to transport lightning up to the Olympus. Thanks to the bridle received as a gift from Athena, it is subsequently tamed by Bellerophon, who uses it as a mount to kill the Chimera. After the hero's death, which happened to have fallen from Pegasus, the winged horse returns among the gods. In the famous singing contest between the Muses and the Pierids, Pegasus had struck Mount Elicona with a hoof, which had grown enormous and threatened heaven after hearing the celestial song of the goddesses. From the point hit by Pegaso's base a spring was born, called Hippocrene, or "source of the horse".
In the same way, Pegasus gave rise to a spring at Trezene. After his exploits, Pegasus takes flight towards the highest part of the sky and turns into a cloud of sparkling stars that have formed a constellation.
With the name of Pegasus several minor mythological figures are defined, all deformations of the Greek Pegasus. In Latin literature, Pliny describes how Pegasi of the birds of Ethiopia with horse heads. Pliny also describes under the same name a horse with wings and horns. For Giulio Solino and Pomponio Mela it would instead be a bird with horse's ears. In general, each figure, mythological or heraldic, corresponding to a winged horse is called Pegasus.

The Hours or Seasons

The Hours, or Seasons, are figures of Greek mythology, daughters of Zeus and of Temi. The Hours were sisters of the Moire and were considered the keepers of Olympus. Originally there were three and symbolized the regular flow of time in the alternation of the seasons (spring, summer and autumn fused together, winter); then a fourth was added (allusion to autumn); in Roman times they ended up with the personification of the real hours, becoming 12 and last 24 hours. The hours are presented in two aspects:

1. As daughters of Themes, the Universal Order, they ensured respect for the moral laws.
2. As gods of nature they presided over the cycle of vegetation.

These two aspects explain their names:

- Eunomia, Legality.
- Diche, Justice. It is presented as "Virgin" and Plato considers this condition to be incorrupt, because it must be "Justice".
- Irene, Peace. The goddess was represented by a young woman carrying, in one hand, an olive branch with cornucopia and in the other Pluto, symbols of that richness and abundance that only peace can give. Altars and statues in Athens and Rome were erected to the goddess. In this last city Vespasiano and Domiziano erected a temple with porticoes and gardens (Temple of Oeace, later considered one of the Imperials Forum). The goddess was also represented on coins.

or:

- Thallus, the spring flowering.
- Auso, the summer luxense.
- Carpo, the autumn fruiting.

The Hours guarded the gates of Zeus's dwelling on Olympus (they opened and closed them, dispersing or accumulating a thick curtain of clouds), they served Hera - who had bred - attacked and detached the horses from his chariot and from that of Elio; they were also part of the procession of Aphrodite - along with the Carites - and Dionysus. The ancients represented them as graceful girls holding a flower or a seedling in their hands, imagining them, however, brown and invisible with reference to the hours of the night; but, except for an alleged marriage of Carpo with Zéfiro, they did not make them the protagonists of any legend.
They honored them with a special cult in Athens (where a temple was consecrated to them), in Argo, in Corinth and in Olympia.

The Nymphs

Greek mythology includes many nymphs, minor deities of nature, whose appearance is of beautiful young girls eternally young. There are many myths about them; these often associate them with satyrs, hence the sexual tendency of nymphomania.

The nymphs (from the Greek word nymfe "maiden future bride") were daughters of Uranus and their myths are linked to greater divinities such as Artemis, Apollo, Poseidon, Demeter, Dionysus, Pan, Hermes or minor gods like Fontus.

There are different types of nymphs, depending on the natural environment in which they live.

They are distinguished in particular:
- Land Nymphs - Epigee
- Aquatic Nymphs - Water tanks
- Celestial Ninfe

They are represented as attractive maidens, virgins of marriageable age. They are beneficial and make nature fertile.

They protect boyfriends who go to bathe in their springs, they inspire human beings, some are also healers of evils and wounds. Lovers of gods and ordinary mortals, the nymphs sing happily in the place consecrated to them. Many demigods were born from their unions with mortals. They represented the forces of nature and especially personified the vital and procreative character, they animated with their invisible presence every manifestation of nature, in particular of the mountains, the waters, the woods, the trees, and by extension also of places, regions, of city. The Nymphs did not enjoy immortality, although Hesiod attributed them an extreme longevity, and remained young forever. The Nymphs did not live in Olympus, even if in the Iliad, when Zeus summoned all the gods in solemn assembly, all the Nymphs are also present.

Prophetic gifts were also attributed to the Nymphs; the gift of healing was the exclusive privilege of the Nymphs of the waters. Among the most famous nymphs, we can mention Eco, the nymph of Mount Elicona; It was he who took the opportunity to utter a word, so Eco could not repeat anything other than the last words spoken by others. Another famous nymph was Eurydice, wife of Orpheus.

The Calypso nymph mentioned in the Odyssey is very well known: she held Ulysses for several years on the island of Ogigia. In Roman mythology, the nymph Egeria was the secret advisor to King Numa Pompilius. They also remember the Naiads who kidnapped the young Argonaut Ila. The Greek nymphs were later assimilated to the Roman divinities of fountains, springs and rivers.

The rituals of offering to the nymphs included sacrifices of lambs and goats, but most of these offerings consisted of milk, oil, honey, fruit and rustic offerings. In the visual arts the nymphs are usually represented as beautiful girls, generally nude and crowned with flowers. The water nymphs in particular are shown as they hold jars or jugs on their heads.

The Earthly Nymphs

The Epigeas are figures of Greek mythology, otherwise called earthly nymphs. Those who live in the mountains and with their song and their joyous games light up the hills are the Oreadis who often take the name from the mountain that hosts them (the Corice lived a cave of Parnassus, the Ditèe the Ditte, the Idèe the Ida) ; perhaps the best known is Eco, Pan's partner, in love with the beautiful Narcissus. The Napee are the nymphs of the wild valleys and meadows where the green of the grass blends with the thousand colors of the flowers; they love the sweet solitude of the wild places but sometimes grant their love to some lucky human being or to some satyr, similar to the Auloniadi that wander in the steep ravines. Alseidi is the name of the inhabitants of the woods that, particularly loved by the hunter Artemis, are part of her sylvan cortege.

The most ancient are considered the Meliadi, inhabitants of the ash trees with warlike characteristics (perhaps because the javelins were built with this wood), born from the drops of blood gushed out following the emanation of Uranus and falls on the Mother Earth, which is fertilized .

The Hamadryas dwell within the virgin bark of the trees and die with them when their life has come to an end or when man knocks them down; their closest sisters, the Dryads, are on the contrary immortal as Eurydike and the beautiful Dafne.

Closer to the civilized world are the Agrostine, protectors of the fields that produce the sustenance necessary for men, the Epimelids, guardians of the flocks, the Cures, unsurpassed nurses, and the Maenads; to these nymphs, followers of Dionysus, god of intoxication, mortal women also joined, who abandoned themselves to ecstasy caused by wine and wild dance.

The Aquatic Nymphs

The nymphs of the waters are the Idrid.

As for the illusory and bewitching depths of water, the oldest nymphs are the three thousand Oceanines "from the thin ankles, which very numerous the earth and the abysses of the sea for every where they also care, bright offspring of goddesses".

Daughters of Oceano and Teti, two titans that symbolize the universal waters and the source before life, gave rise to all the rivers that bathe and revive the earth, including the Acheloo, the major river god of Greece, capable of changing the his own form (as in a challenge against Herakles for Deianira's hand when he turned into a bull, a dragon and an ox).

Stige "among them is the greatest of all", inhabitant of the main infernal stream whose waters can make immortal (Achilles was dipped in its current, kept for a heel that for this remained vulnerable); the gods swear on her, and he who stains himself with perjury for a year "lies without breath; nor can he ever be near the ambrosia and nectar of food and a fatal torpor envelops him "then" for nine years he is deprived of the living gods, and never attends council or banquets ". Other daughters of Oceano are Kalypso, a lover of Odysseus, Metis goddess of wisdom who performed different metamorphoses before allowing herself to Zeus, Tyche, lady of fortune and Perseide, from which queens and sorceresses such as Kirke, Pasifae and Medea will descend.

Another of these nymphs, Doris, joining Nereo "the old man of the sea", divinity symbolizing the calm sea, son of Ponto and Gaia and thus preceding the birth of the Olimpi, will give life to the beautiful Nerito and the fifty Nereids. Of these, the most famous are: Tethys, mother of Achilles, Galatea, beloved by the Cyclops Polyphemus, and Amphitryte, who will become the bride of the next sea god, Posidone, the god with the turquoise hair that carries the trident. From this union will be born Rhodos and Tritone, father of the Tritons who walk the sea playing the whips to arouse or calm the storms. Euripides nell'Andromaca suggests that the marine nymphs "Zeus has given an existence and a dwelling far from men, settling at the ends of the earth. It is there that they live, the heart free from troubles, in the islands of the Blessed, on the banks of the deep vortexes of the ocean, lucky heroes for whom this fertile soil brings thriving and sweet harvest three times a year.

How not to approach this description to the myriad of enchanted islands present in various traditions, where heroes can stay after death? The inhabitants of the terrestrial waters, take the name of Naiadi (from the Greek "flow" or "source") and are called alternately daughters of Ocean, Zeus or the river god closest to their home.

These creatures are divided into various species depending on the place they live: the Potameids animate the crystalline waters of the rivers, the Pegee or Crenee the clear springs arising from the unfathomable depths of the earth and the Limniadi the stagnant pools that seem to guard secret arcana. Other girls who live in a small island among the waves are the Sirens ("the desired" or "who bind"), those who were Nymphs of the earth and that, to be able to search even on the water their playmate, Persephone, kidnapped by god of the underground world of the dead, turned into living beings inhabited by the seas.

They had a wonderful voice that had the power to attract the sailors who heard it; only Orpheus and Odysseus managed to pass unharmed at their rock. An episode concerning the nymphs of the waters is that of Hylas, the splendid young man, lover and squire of Herakles who had embarked with the Argonauts.

During a stop on an island he was sent to stock up on water and soon saw a spring in a low ground; in the midst of the water the

Nymphs intertwined a choir, the sleepless nymphs, the fearsome goddesses of the country, Eunica, and Malide, and Nicaea look of spring. "They fell in love with the beautiful boy, and when he bent over the mirror of the water seized him and carried him to the depths, where with sweet words they cheered him up. Herakles, worried, started looking for his companion and three times shouted his name, but the young man's voice seemed to come from a great distance, and never again saw him again.

Alseadi

Inhabitants of the woods were part of the sylvan cortege of Artemis Diana. Often with variously colored veils on the naked body.

They appeared in the form of young and beautiful girls to whom no man could resist. There were, however, some "good" nymphs, as told by the myth of Heracles, which with magical filters, composed mainly of the leaves of some plants useful for healing wounds or traumas, even psychological ones, gave protection and passion to strangers.

The most famous were Callisto and her younger sister Anthea, sentimentally linked to Artemis, goddess of hunting.

They are said to have silver hair.

Oreadi

Nymphs of the mountains divided into:
- Ideas, which inhabited Mount Ida.
- The Peliades, who lived on Mount Pelion.
- The Ditee, who lived in Mount Ditte.
- The Coricc, who lived in the cave of Corice at the foot of Mount Parnassus.

Perhaps the best known of the Oreadis is Eco, the inhabitant of Mount Helicon, a companion of Pan, who fell in love with Narcissus.

According to Ovid, Zeus noting Eco's aptitude for gossip, urged her to entertain his wife Hera so as to distract her from her stealthy loves. However, he was aware of the deception, and he punished her by removing the use of the word and condemning her to repeat only the last words that were addressed or heard.

The nymph fell madly in love with Narcissus, but not being able to confess his love, he could only repeat the last words he spoke. Exasperated by this attitude Narciso fled from Eco, never finding himself ever again. The desperate nymph began to look for him everywhere, and from the pain she let herself go hungry. Only her voice remained of her and the pity gods transformed her into a rock.

These nymphs were associated with Artemis, a deity that hunted preferably between the mountains and the precipices.

Napee

Nymphs of the valleys and meadows. They loved loneliness, but sometimes they had relationships of love with some heroes, from which they demanded absolute fidelity.

They were often harassed and chased by Pan, or threatened by the Faunal procurers and the Satyrs, who pursued them and ended up bending them to their lascivious cravings: they did not derive their name from the Greek word nose, which means covered place, as they are the woods where Fauni and Satiri roamed like them, protected and predacious, while the Napee had the habit of dancing, with nimble foot, on the fresh grass of the meadows and insidious thickets.

Auloniad

They are the particular type of nymphs, subgenus of the Dryads and very similar to the Alseidae, which could be found in river valleys and mountain pastures, often in the company of the god Pan, the Lord of Nature. When they are near the woods they are in correlation with the Napee. Eurydice, for which the singer Orfeo of her in love traveled in the dark Hades, is often indicated to be one of them, or in any case in association with the Auloniades; she found death in the valley of the river Peneo in Thessaly, in an attempt to escape from Aristeo, the beautiful son of the god Apollo whose desire to possess her was interrupted by the intervention of a poisonous snake that bit the young girl to an ankle. Aristeo was the son of Apollo and the nymph Cyrene. Aristeo's birth took place in Libya, where Apollo had brought Cirene after the abduction. Ermes assisted in giving birth and his nymphs took care of him by teaching him the art of pastoralism, such as making cheese, beekeeping and the cultivation of the olive tree. Educated by the Chiron centaur for war and hunting, he dedicated his life to raising bees and becoming a shepherd. Once he became an adult, he married Autonoe and from this union Actaeon was born. He moved to Beozia where he learned hunting techniques, medicine and how to keep flocks.

He fell in love with the nymph Eurydice and the same day that she married Orpheus, he tried to make it his before her husband and in the pursuit that followed Eurydice succeeded several times to escape, until accidentally stepped on a poisonous snake that with its bite the He killed. In revenge, the other nymphs destroyed his hives.

Cyrene, his mother, then advised Aristeo to appease their anger by offering them cattle, leaving them on the ground and returning to the place after nine days. So he did and on his return he found a swarm of bees in the carcasses, which repaid him extensively for the loss he had suffered. Aristeo was honored as a god in many places in Greece for having taught men beekeeping, cheese production and pastoralism.

Maenads

Also called Baccanti, they were women in the grip of ecstatic frenzy and possessed by Dionysus, the god of life force; in fact, more properly, the maenads were the mythological followers of the god, while women who historically have worshiped the god are called "Bacchae". The term Menadi derives from Menio, king of Orcomeno, a Beota city near Tebe.

According to the story contained in "The metamorphoses" by Antonino Liberale, the three laborious daughters of Menio (called Menadi) were disinterested in the cult of Dionysus. The latter, however, irritated, invaded the sisters and led them to insanity, infanticide and homophage.

The story ends with the intervention of Hermes who turns the women, now become uncontainable Baccanti, in three nocturnal birds (bat, owl and owl) .Dress of nebris or other animal skins, with a crown of ivy or oak or fir on his head , they celebrated the god singing, dancing and wandering like animals for mountains and forests. They usually stirred the thyrsus, that is, a pike enveloped by ivy on top. Greek mythology tells that the Maenads accompanied the god Dionysus in his travels, also constituting a department of his army on his journey to India. The cult practiced by the Maenads is the background to one of the most important tragedies of Euripides entitled "The Bacchae".

From the Maenads and from the myth of Dionysus one derives its origins from a cult, probably mystical, defined as "menadism", in which there was also a ritual characterized by the consumption of raw meats (homophagia). In classical iconography the maenads are portrayed as the object of desire of the satyrs in the arms of which they are often depicted.

- The Bacchae are also named in the legend of Orpheus and Eurydice: Orpheus, after having lost for the second time Euridice, wanders through the woods, where he meets a group of Bacchae, who invite Orpheus to celebrate with them. But Orpheus, after the death of

Eurydice no longer wants female companies, and the Bacchae, offenses, kill him.

Thus Orpheus can descend to the underworld and reunite with his beloved Eurydice.

Dryads

Nymphs of the oaks, as revealed by their name (dryas, oak) daughters of Nerèo and Dori, although later the term was used to indicate all the nymphs of trees in general. The dryads were nymphs who lived in the woods and embodied their strength and vegetative luxuriance. Unlike hamadryas, they did not make bodies with trees, nor did they die with them, but they could move freely, dance and unite even with mere mortals. They were depicted as beautiful and young women, with the lower part of the person ending in a sort of arabesque that imitated a tree trunk.

The upper part instead highlighted a certain beauty and radiance. Among the Dryads one remembers in particular Driope. Driope was a princess who was transformed into a nymph. In some sources it is daughter of Eurito, king of Ecàlia, in others of Driope, king of the Driopi. Driope was originally a young woman who later became a rural nymph. In the myth he keeps the flocks for his father, together with the Amadriadi. She was one of the many women Apollo was abusing. The myth tells that the god turned into a turtle to bring the Amadriads and Driope closer together.

When the nymph took the animal, it turned into a snake, letting the nymphs escape, so that they could possess Driope in peace. Later Driope married Andremone, but from the relationship with the god was born Anfisso, founder of the city of Eta, where he erected a temple to the god Apollo. The myth has several versions, all coinciding until the birth of Anfisso. In one version, Driope becomes a priestess of Apollo, in the temple of Eta, until the Amadriadi transform her into one of them, leaving a poplar in her place. Instead, the most common version sees her involuntarily committing a sacrilege against the Amadriade Lotide. Driope would have gone near a lake with her sister, Iole, and her son, to offer garlands to the local nymphs.

Nearby there was a lotus plant, from which she cut a flower to let her son play. Blood began to flow from the flowers, as that was the plant in which Lotide had turned to escape Priapus, who wanted to rape her. After a while, Driope began to turn into a lotus in turn. Shortly before losing his full human appearance, he greeted his sister, father and husband, rushed to his aid, and begged them to take care of his little son, who was still in his arms. He asked that it be entrusted to a nurse, and that it was brought near the tree where it was being transformed, to teach him the love for flowers and plants, recommending to respect them because in each one could be the body of an Amadriade.

In the Aeneid Driope, already a nymph, he joins Fauno (a character not well known, almost certainly an Etruscan, homonym of the Italic god), from whom he has the gritty hero Tarquito, allied with Turn in the war against the Trojans and destined to end up victim of Aeneas. According to other authors, Driope is also the mother of the god Pan, given by the god Hermes. Legend has it that the nymph fled before the appearance of this child with a goat's body. Driope is the nymph linked to the Capelvenere plant.

Hamadryads

They are nymphs that live inside the trees; they are a special kind of Dryads, which are themselves a particular type of nymphs. They are partly associated with the Querquetulanae, the Roman nymphs of the oak grove. Hamadryas are born tied to a certain tree; some believe it is the real tree, that is to say it is a personification of it, while the normal dryads are spiritual entities or divinities of the trees. If the tree is dead, even the madrid associated with it dies, and that is why the gods punish mortals who allow themselves to harm trees without any reason. University of Naucrati lists eight hamadryas, daughters of Oxylo (son of Orea) and his sister Hamadryas:
- Karya (walnut, hazel or chestnut).
- Balanos/Balanus (oak).
- Kraneia (cornel or cherry).
- Morea (mulberry).
- Aigeiros (black poplar).
- Ptelea (elm).
- Ampelos (vitis vinifera, deriving from the name of Ampelo, the adolescent satyr loved by Dionysus).
- Syke (ficus).

Callimachus in his "Hymn to Delos" tells us that the disposition and the temperament of these deities varies according to the type of tree placed under their protection, paying in tears when the leaves fall or in shouts of raucous joy with the arrival of the spring rains on the young green foliage. Amadriade Carya (from which the genus Carya takes its name) following a relationship with Zeus, has generated Dirio, the god of poisonous plants.
Then there are legends that describe the vindictive power that these nymphs were able to express to those who threatened their trees, other stories tell us about the punishment that fell on those who had cut off their trees without permission or who moved away from the prayers assigned to these deities, being regarded as intermediaries between mortals and immortals.

Epimelidi

Nninfc protcctors of apple and apple trees.
It is said that, in the land of the Messapians, near the place
called the Sacred Stones, the Epimelid nymphs who led the
dances appeared and then (after the appearance of the dancing
nymphs) the messapi children, after leaving the flocks, while
they watched the dances said that they themselves knew how to
lead them even better.
The Nymphs did not like this speech and raced between the
parties, for some time on the superiority of dancing: the
children, thinking of competing with mortal women similar to
them, certainly did not know that they competed with divine
beings.
The children had a simple, crude way of dancing, like that of the
shepherds: but to the nymphs all things often increased
elegance. Let the children win, so they said to them: "Children,
you have challenged the Epimelid nymphs; therefore foolish
(crazy), because you have been vanquished you will be
punished ".
And the children in that place where they had stopped, near the
temple of the nymphs, were transformed into trees, and today, at
night, a sad voice comes from the forest, almost to complain.
The place appeals to the Nymphs and children.

Dafnaie

Nymphs of the bay tree.

Among the Dafnaie we remember in particular Dafne.

Dafne, daughter of Gaea and of the river Peneo (or according to others of the river Lacone), was a young and delightful nymph who lived quietly spending her time delighting in the quiet of the woods and the pleasure of hunting when her life was distorted by the whim of two deities: Apollo and Eros. Legend has it that Apollo, proud of having killed the monstrous snake Python, met Eros while he was intending to forge a new bow, mocked him and the fact that he had never performed actions worthy of glory.

The god of love, deeply wounded by the words of Apollo, flew to the top of Mount Parnassus and there he prepared his revenge: he took two arrows, a very sharp and golden, destined to give birth to the passion, which he threw violently into the heart of Apollo and another, popped and lead, destined to repel love, which he threw into the heart of Daphne. From that day on, Apollo began to wander desperately through the woods in search of the nymph, until he could not find it. At his sight, Daphne, escaped fearful and to no avail the pleas of the god who cried out his love and his divine origins to try to impress the young girl.

Daphne, terrified, escaped through the woods. But he realized that his race was vain, as Apollo was about to reach, invoked his mother Gaea, begging her to change her appearance because so much pain and fear was getting her. His mother, Gea, listened to his prayer and so began to slow down his daughter's race to stop her and at the same time to transform her body: her hair changed into light fronds; his arms rose high towards the sky, becoming flexible branches; his graceful body was covered with bark; his delicate feet turned into sturdy roots and his tear-stained face vanished at the top of the tree. Daphne was transformed into a graceful and strong tree that took the name of Lauro (from the Greek dafne = laurel). The transformation had taken place under the eyes of a desperate Apollo, embracing the trunk in the hope of being able to find the sweet Dafne. In the end, the god, considering his attempts as useless, proclaimed with great clarity that the laurel plant would have been sacred to his cult and a sign of glory to be placed on the head of the victors. Even today, in memory of Daphne, it is common to proclaim the best among men, those capable of thrilling enterprises, with the head encircled by a laurel wreath. There is also an alternative version of the first story that presents us as a mortal Dafne, daughter of Amicla; passionate about hunting, she was firmly determined to preserve her virginity. He walked the mountains with his companions, huntresses like her, living under the protection of Artemis. Leucippo (the "white stallion"), who fell in love with her, dressed up as a woman and joined the group of hunters; at this point Apollo, who was greedy, decided to unmask the deception by inspiring the group of young women the desire to get wet in a spring.

Leucippo was forced to undress and was therefore discovered (similar to the myth of Callisto); only the intervention of the gods, who took care to make it invisible, could prevent the young man from making a tragic end. Apollo in the ensuing bustle tried to kidnap Dafne, who however managed to escape him and, at her prayer, was transformed by Zeus into a laurel.

This partly different story, narrated by the Hellenist poet Partenio in his "Erotica Pathemata" (the pains of love), turned out to be less and less familiar, also because the art of the Renaissance exalted the story as described by Ovid. The myth of Apollo and Daphne has been variously examined as a battle between chastity (Daphne) and sexual desire (Apollo). As Apollo pursues for lust Daphne's lust, so this is saved through his metamorphosis and confinement in the laurel tree which can be seen as an act of eternal chastity. Daphne is forced to sacrifice her body and become a plant as her only chance of escape from the pressures of Apollo's constant sexual desires.

The god finally welcomes the eternal chastity of Daphne and creates a crown from its branches, transforming his symbol of chastity into a cultural symbol for him and all the other poets and musicians.

Naiad

Nninfe who presided over all the sweet waters of the earth and possessed healing and prophetic faculties.
Endowed with great longevity, but mortal, they were known for their benevolence toward the human world, and by virtue of the vital forces of water they were honored as the nurses of plants, animals, and men. For this reason they considered themselves as nurses of Dionysus and Demeter. They dance in happy choruses in the company of Satyrs and Sileni, cultivating music, poetry and the art of divination.

The Satyrs - The satyr is a mythical male figure, companion of Pan and Dionysus, who inhabits woods and mountains.
It is a minor deity, personification of the fertility and vital force of nature, connected with the Dionysian cult. In ancient Roman religion it is known as "faun". Satyrs are generally portrayed as bearded human beings with horns, tail and goat legs. Their appearance gradually lost, with the passage of time, some animal attribute. They are portrayed as lascivious beings, often dedicated to wine, dancing with nymphs and playing the flute. Sometimes they are depicted with a conspicuous erection. Their main exponent was Silenus, a minor deity associated (like Hermes and Priapus) with fertility. In Greek mythology it is said that the satyrs were great flute players who enchanted with their music. This instrument was the invention of the goddess Athena, who threw it, annoyed by the way in which it deformed her cheeks while she was playing it. The satyr Marsia picked it up (and was beaten by the goddess for his disrespectful gesture) and began to play it with incredible mastery, so that, pretending to be able to play a "divine" music, challenged Apollo (in other versions it was instead the god to challenge Marsia, jealous of his skill) who promised to take him up with him on Olympus if his music had been better than his own, while otherwise the satyr would have been punished. The Muses would have decreed the winner. The satyr, however, could not stand the challenge when Apollo began to accompany the lyre with the

song, since he could not sing while playing the flute. Triumphant, the god dispose of the satyr and skinned him alive in the presence of the Muses.

The Silenes - The Silenians are figures of Greek mythology, minor deities of the woods, of wild and lascivious nature, related to the centaurs and enemies of agriculture, very often assimilated to the satyrs, so much so that the term silenus is also used to indicate a satyr elderly, also called papposilenes. Silenus is the god of the trees, son of Pan and of a nymph. From the appearance of a burly, bald, furry senior, often depicted with animalistic attributes, he had the gift of extraordinary wisdom, despised earthly goods, and even had the gift of divination. King Midas captured him just to force him (successfully, according to some versions of the myth) to reveal his powers that gave boundless wisdom and the ability to predict the future. It is also said that the sage Silenus was the educator of Dionysus youth; after having played his role in accompanying the young god during the journey of growth, he would have completely abandoned himself to the habit of drinking. It was believed that he participated in the sacred banquets to Dionysus by presenting himself on the back of an ass and is often seen as part of the Dionysian tiaso.

The origin of the Naiads varies both according to the mythographs and according to the legends. Homer, for example, refers to them by calling them "Daughters of Zeus", elsewhere they are linked to the lineage of Oceanus, more commonly they are simply daughters of the god of the river in which they live. Whatever their origin, however, it is certain that the Naiads were characters familiar to the Hellenistic imagination. In fact, not only did each watercourse have an associated Naiad but these characters were also very often used to explain some phenomena, thus acquiring a very important function in local legends. It was believed that they had healing powers: the sick people drank the water from their sources or immersed themselves, though more rarely; this act was, in fact, considered sacrilegious and one could risk incurring anger and revenge of the goddesses, which manifested themselves in the form of particular illnesses. In Rome, Nero himself, after immersing himself in the source of the March, was seized by a paralysis and a fever that left him a few days later. The cult of the Naiads - who were considered beneficial gods of health - was more popular among the peasants, who honored them with offers of flowers, fruit and milk. They are distinguished by the aquatic deities, which represented the same rivers, and by the ancient spirits that inhabited the calm waters of the marshes, ponds and lagoons or lakes, as for the pre-historic Lerna in Argolida. The Naiads are associated with fresh waters, such as the Oceanines for the salty waters and the Mediterranean Nereids; however, since the Greeks thought that the waters of the world constituted a single system, which penetrated from the sea into the deep cavernous spaces of the earth, there was sometimes some overlap. Arethusa, the nymph of a spring, was able to move through underground currents from the Peloponnese to resurface somewhere in Sicily. In ancient texts, the Naiads were often used to give prestige to the most important families. Many genealogies originally present a Naiad; for example, the wife of Erichthonius, Prassitea who begat Pandion; the wife of Endimione, mother of Etolo; that of Icarius, Peribea who generated Penelope.

The Naiads are represented in the nude artistic works, splendid with youth, crowned with reeds, pouring water from an urn holding a shell or a horn from which water gushes. They were distinguished in:

- Potameidi, nymphs of rivers. They are represented as attractive maidens, virgins of marriageable age. They are beneficial and make nature fertile. They protect boyfriends who go to bathe in their springs, they inspire human beings, some are also healers of ills. Simple mortals who however live an extremely long life, lovers of gods and common mortals, the nymphs sing happily happy in the place consecrated to them.

- Pegee, nymphs of the springs, immortal. The name seems to derive from the Pegea waterfall; the Pegee nymphs were responsible for the abduction of Ila: one of the nymphs took it and pulled it to the water to kiss it, then dragging it into the river.

- Crenee, fountain nymphs, immortals. They sometimes take the form of fish or mossy rocks.
- Limniadi, nymphs of lakes and ponds.
- Eleadi, nymphs of the swamps. The Eleadi are a shy breed of aquatic reptiles that have been elevated to the status of humanoid by ancient magic. They live mainly along the marshes and streams of Teti where they live on plants with river fish and birds. As a people, heleads are basically solitary and shy, they rarely interact with other races. When they interact with humans, they do it as guides or as trawlers. Usually these nymphs live in hidden villages, which are located in the middle of the marshes on artificial islands, protected by aquatic monsters. The society of the Eleadi does not recognize the difference between the sexes and the social classes. They have multiple survival skills, but few artists, for this they are greedy for jewelry and shiny objects, especially gold.

In the Roman religion, these nymphs took the name of Camene, archaic deities of the springs, and they were four:
- Egeria
- Carmenta
- Antevorta
- Postvorta

They were sometimes given prophetic and more generally "inspiring" faculties. Because of this complex nature, the figure and the myth of Camene articulated over time. First of all, they were the protective divinities of the archaic fireplace, symbolically assimilated to the city: so the first of them, Egeria, was inspired by the second king of Rome, Numa Pompilio, of the Sabina lineage and promoter of concord among the first Roman tribes (remember the rats' sabine). In imagining nature, it is worth bearing in mind the assonance between Egeria, ager (the land to be cultivated) and agger (the defense embankment): the figure that emerges is that of an archaic and powerful female deity, born cults of the earth, which inspires the king of the new city wisdom, harmony and pacification.

We are between the seventh and sixth centuries BC Antevorta (looking ahead) and Postvorta (looking backwards) were personifications related to childbirth, invoked so that the fetus would present itself in the right position (with the head forward), and be saved if it appeared on the contrary. More than names of single deities were probably above all appellations, and connected the archaic and protective nature of the women of the deity to the oracular one. Through Carmenta then - from the most pronounced oracular qualities, and from which the term "carmen" was derived, (song, epic story, poetry), they became the Roman personification of the Muses. At the Camene, Numa Pompilius had consecrated the wood at the source of Egeria, outside Porta Capena.

Nereids

Sca nymphs, daughters of Nereus and the Doric Oceanina.
They were considered immortal and benevolent creatures. They
were part of the procession of the god of the sea Poseidon along
with the Tritons and were represented as girls with hair adorned
with pearls, riding dolphins or sea horses. The most famous
Nereids are Amphitrite, bride of Poseidon, Galatea, loved by the
shepherd Aci and the Cyclops Polyphemus and Teti, mother of
the hero Achilles.

Nereus - Nereus is a primitive marine deity of Greek
mythology, son of Pontus and Gaia. He is portrayed as an old
sage who foretold events, just and benevolent, called by Homer
"old man of the sea". Nereo lives at the bottom of the Aegean
Sea and has the faculty to take different forms, in particular that
of snake, water and fire, and to predict the future, typical
characteristics of many marine deities. He was the one who
foretold in Paris all the evils that would come from the
abduction of Helen of Troy. Eracle managed to get from him the
necessary information to reach the Garden of the Hesperides to
collect the golden apples. She was the husband of the little
ocean Doride, from whom she had the Nereids, including Alice
and Teti, the latter mother of Achilles, with whom she lived in a
cave in the depths of the sea. Perhaps he had a son, Nerito, and
therefore a brother of the fifty Nereids. From her sisters and her
parents she had inherited a beautiful aspect, so much so that
Aphrodite fell in love during the period when the goddess lived
in the sea. When Aphrodite had to go up to Olympus, she
wanted to take Nerito with her, but the young man preferred to
stay with his father Nereus and his sisters, the Nereids. The
goddess then turned it into a shell. This metamorphosis is
sometimes attributed to the jealousy that Elios (the Sun) felt for
the speed with which Nerite, loved by Poseidon, followed the
god among the waves.

Hesiod in his Theogony, he reports a list of 51 names, while Homer in the Iliad cites 33 Nereids who, with their sister Teti, complied with Achilles' pain for the death of Patroclus. According to both, however, there were fifty in number. Pseudo-Apollodorus, author of the Bibliotheca provides us with a list of 45 names while Hyginus, author of the second century of the Fabulae, a list of 49 names (actually 48, when taking into account a name repeated), other late mythographers also speak of 100 marine nymphs, the first of which was Amphitrite, direct emanation of Doride.

The following is the list of Nereid names as shown in the comparison of all available sources:

- Actea - Actea is the nymph of the shore, the inhabitant of the sea coast.
- Agave.
- Alia - Hesiod defines her as "lovable", while Homer "with big eyes".
- Alimede - Alimede was a nymph of the Mediterranean Sea, with a docile and gentle character. Although sometimes she was portrayed as a beautiful girl, in some places in Greece she was portrayed as a half human figure and half with the appearance of a fish.
- Amatea.
- Anfinome.
- Anfitoe.
- Amphitrite - It was a symbol of the force of the sea. The legend attributes to her husband Poseidon that she would have long repulsed until she let herself be persuaded by the insistence of a dolphin who convinced her to marry the unattractive Poseidon. From the union of the two born three sons: Tritone, Rodo and Bentesicima. Triton had a conch horn that calmed the storms with its sound and announced the arrival of the sea god. Very well known for the help he gave to Jason and the Argonauts in finding the route to follow. Triton was depicted with the upper half human and the lower one in the shape of a fish, all the skin was green. Rodo was also a lover of Helios. He also gave the name to the

island of Rhodes and its inhabitants. Bentesicima, the wave goddess, was only one of the most dangerous aspects of Amphitrite. Poseidon, the god of the seas, had from a relationship with Chion a son named Eumolpus; the girl, fearful of the possible fury of her father, threw the child into the water and Poseidon, guiding the flow of water as he pleased, made sure that the infant would arrive in Ethiopia from Bentesicima, to breed him. Later, the husband of Bentesicima gave Eumolpus one of his two daughters as his wife. Amphitrite is represented sitting on a chariot shaped like a shell pulled by dolphins and surrounded by Tritons and Nereids some of which hold the reins, while others blow in the sea horns to announce the arrival of the goddess who with a scepter of gold in her hand commanded the waves.

In Roman mythology, it is called Salacia.

- Apseude.
- Aretusa - Was faithful companion of Artemis. Once to cool off after a hunt, he bathed in the river Alpheus, who fell in love with the nymph and took the human form. Artemis, recalled by the cries of help after turning Aretusa into a spring, plunged her underground and brought it back to the island of Ortigia. Alfeo, not at all discouraged, summed up the aquatic forms and could thus join the nymph. Aretusa is represented in the Syracusan currencies considered to be among the most beautiful in the world, from its head surrounded by darting dolphins (this motif also appears in Italian currencies of five hundred lire).
- Autonoe.
- Goblet.
- Calipso - Calipso is an Oceanina, or a Nereid, but on its genealogy the sources are divided:
  - ➤ Some consider her as the daughter of Atlas and Pleione: the legend accepted by Homer.
  - ➤ Daughter of Elio (the Sun) and of Perseide, then sister of Eete and Circe.

> According to Hesiod, he was one of the Oceanines, daughters of the Titan Oceano and Titanide Teti.
> Finally, it appears also in the list of Nereids, the daughters of Nereus and Doris.

According to the story of the Odyssey of Homer it was, instead, daughter of Atlas and lived on the island of Ogigia, which the authors place in the Mediterranean West and which is similar to the peninsula of Ceuta, in front of Gibraltar but also a cave on the shore at the sea, on the island of Gozo, it is referred to as the home of Calypso. One day Ulysses, escaped from the vortex of Charybdis, landed on the island and Calypso fell in love with it. The Odyssey tells how she loved him and kept him with her, according to Homer, for seven years (according to Pseudo-Apollodoro five and only one according to Igino) offering him in vain immortality, which the hero insistently refused. Ulysses kept in his heart the desire to return to Ithaca, and did not allow himself to be seduced. Calypso lived in a deep cave, with many rooms, which opened onto natural gardens, a sacred wood with large trees and springs that flowed through the grass. She spent her time spinning, weaving, with the slaves, also nymphs, who sang while they worked. The tears of Ulysses were welcomed by Athena, who, sorry for her protégé, asked Zeus to intervene. The god then sent Hermes to convince Calypso to let him leave and she reluctantly consented. He gave them timber to build a raft and provisions for the trip. He also indicated to him on which stars to adjust the navigation. The legends after the Odyssey ascribe to Ulisse and Calypso a son, called Latino, more often considered as the son of Circe; sometimes it is said that they had two sons, Nausitoo and Nausinoo, whose names remind the ship. Finally, Ausone, the eponym of Ausonia, is attributed to him as a son.

- Callianassa.
- Callinira.
- Class.
- Cimatolege.

- Cimo.
- Cimodoce - the one that calms "the waves on the foggy sea and the breaths of the divine winds". In the Aeneid, when the ships of Aeneas are transformed into nymphs by Cybele, the one in which the hero finds himself takes the form of Cimodocea, which, more than the others, proved to have fluency of language. Grab the stern of the ship with your right hand Aeneas and swimming with his left, informed him of what was happening at the Trojan camp. He urged him to hurry up and land so that he could attack first, and he helped him in that direction by giving a push to the ship on which the hero stood, giving it a strong speed.
- Cimotoe.
- Climene - Wife of Prometheus and mother of Deucalion.
- Chorus.
- Cranto.
- Dero.
- Dessamene.
- Dynamene.
- Dione.
- Doride - According to a tradition, he joined Zeus and generated a son from him, the river god Scamander, which ran around the Trojan stronghold.
In Greek mythology, Scamander was the name of several characters, one was a god of a river, the other was his nephew. Scamander (or Xanto) is a river god, son of Zeus and Doride. His father gave him the honor of celebrating the young women who went to bathe in his waters after the wedding. As soon as he got out of the water, Scamandro came out of his bed and accompanied them to his palace. During the Trojan war, when Patroclus died, Achille's close friend, killed by a spear thrown at him by Hector, Achilles, having returned to the battlefield, massacred Trojans and Troy allies; after having killed so many young people in the plain of Troy, not having succeeded in attacking and

killing his greatest and hated rival Hector, he turned against the enemies who tried, to escape his fury, to take refuge on the opposite bank of the Scamander river, to find shelter and save from the sword of the angry Greek hero. Achilles, still burning with rage and anxiety of revenge, threw himself into the river and began to chase the fugitives inside the water, making slaughter, leaving weapons, shields and armor to clutter the river and the water of the same river containing corpses with severed heads and left with the helmets to float on the surface; soon there were chilling islands of corpses and the god of the river waters, disdained by the carnage, throws his waters against the Greek hero, trying to overwhelm him, taking away his sight and his breath. Achilles, weighed down by the armor, struggles with all his strength, coming to understand in the end that he is about to drown; is finally saved from the intervention of Vulcan that drains the waters of the river with a tremendous rain of fire that allows the hero to save his life and escape forever safe and sound to the fury of the Scamander god who tried to kill him to avenge his the death of the infinites killed by the fury and the iron of the young Greek hero.

- Doto.
- Eion.
- Erato.
- Eucrante.
- Eudia.
- Eudore.
- Eulimene.
- Eumolpe.
- Eunice.
- Eupompe.
- Evagore.
- Avoid them.
- Ferusa.
- Galatea - Cyclops Polyphemus fell in love with her, but Galatea loved Aci, the beautiful son of Fauno.

Polyphemus, driven by jealousy, killed Aci, who was then changed to a source. The myth tells that Galatea was in love with Aci, a beautiful young man, and that the Cyclops Polyphemus, envious of the young man and in turn in love with the nymph, one day tried to lure her with the sound of his flute. Not having succeeded in his intent, surprised the pair of lovers, he infuriated an enormous boulder that caught up, killing him, Aci. As told in the Metamorphoses of Ovid, Galatea, to keep his love alive, he transformed the blood of Aci into a spring and he himself became a river god.

- Galena.
- Glauce.
- Glauconome.
- Ianassa.
- Ianira.
- Iera.
- Ion.
- Ipponoe.
- Ippotoe.
- Iresia.
- Laomedia
- Liagore.
- Limnory.
- Lisianassa.
- Melite - He joined Heracles on the island of Scheria.
- Menippe.
- Mera.
- Nao.
- Nausitoe.
- Nemerte.
- Neomeris.
- Nesea - She was the nurse of Aristaeus and her mother's companion, the nymph Cyrene.
- Neso.
- Orizia.
- Panope.

- Pasitea.
- Plessaure.
- Polinome.
- Pontomedusa.
- Pontoporeia.
- Prote.
- Proto.
- Protomedia.
- Psamatea - Semi-divinity of Greek mythology and specifically the goddess of sand. Joining Eaco generated Foco, who became an adult and was killed by his half-brothers Telamone and Peleo by jealousy. The nymph then began to persecute her son's murderers, and her anger was only appeased by the prayers of her sister Teti, who had married Peleus in the meantime. When Eaco decided to seduce her, Psamate turned into a seal and tried in vain to escape. The man reached her and from their embrace came Foco, who became the king's favorite. Later, Foco was killed by his elder brothers Telamone and Peleo, sons of Eaco's first bed with Endeide. But fratricide was discovered, and the two escaped from Aegina. According to Antonino Liberale, Psamate wanted revenge and unleashed a monstrous wolf against Peleus, who in the meantime had married another Nereid, Teti. The animal accidentally met on its own path the herds of cows that Thetis had brought as a dowry to her husband, and he satiated. When the two spouses arrived, the wolf, satollo, clumsily tried to throw himself at Peleus. Thetis then turned the animal into a stone, which would still be in that place, between Locride and Phocis. Ovid tells, instead, that Peleus, when he faced the wolf, prayed to Psamate to obtain forgiveness, but to no avail. It was then Teti who interceded for his spouse, appeasing his sister's wrath. The wolf, however, did not stop and, after having torn the throat of the last heifer, would have jumped on Peleus, if it had not been the same Psamate to turn it into a marble statue. According to Euripides, Psamate

later married Proteus, king of Egypt, to whom he gave two sons: a male, Theoclyndine, and a female, Eido, who inherited the gift of prophecy from his grandfather Nereus and later assumed the name of Teonoe.

- Sao.
- Speio.
- Talia.
- Temisto.
- Teti - It was the most beautiful of the Nereids and had the gift of metamorphosis that helped to increase its appeal. Bride of Peleus and mother of Achilles, also called Tethys to distinguish her from the homonymous titanessa. Zeus and Poseidon courted her, but when they heard from an oracle that the Nereid would spawn a son stronger than her father, they pulled back. Peleus declared his love to Tetide, who tried to escape him by turning into fire, water, wind and various animals, but always in vain, because each time the hero managed to hold her close to him. In the end the nymph yielded and married Peleus in a grandiose ceremony in which all the deities took part, less Eris who had not been invited, from whom the goddess' revenge threw a pome taken from the garden of the Hesperides, object later of the judgment of Paris. The apple of discord or apple of discord is, according to the myth, the apple thrown by Eris, the goddess of discord, on the table where the banquet was held in honor of the marriage of Peleus and Tethys. The goddess, to take revenge on the lack of invitation to the party, engraved on the apple the phrase "To the Most Beautiful", thus causing a furious quarrel between Hera, queen of gods, Aphrodite, goddess of beauty, and Athena, daughter of Zeus. Zeus refrained from pronouncing the judgment on who was the most beautiful. The opinion of Paride, prince of Troia, was then asked, to which the three goddesses promised several rewards: to give them their respects, Athena promised that he would never lose a war and that he would give him immense powers. Paride, however,

chose as the winner Aphrodite, who had promised him the love of Helen, the most beautiful woman on earth. This will be the triggering cause of the Trojan war, an event to which the epic poems of the Trojan cycle will be dedicated, including the Iliad and the Odyssey. Thetis gave Peleus a son, Achilles, but the marriage was not happy and the day ended when the nymph was surprised by her husband while trying to make his son immortal by placing him on a fire. Peleus moved the child away, fearing that his wife wanted to kill him: the Nereid did not forgive him for that intrusion and left, entrusting his son to Chiron to educate him. Having learned from an oracle that Achilles would die in the Trojan war, Teti hid him from the king of Lycomedes of Scyrus: Achilles grew up at the court of this king under a female identity, which did not prevent him from forming a family with the princess Deidamia, from whom she had Neoptolemus. When the Trojan war broke out, Ulysses, who knew of the plan of Thetis, went to Scyros and with a stratagem forced Achilles to reveal his true identity, so that Teti had to resign himself to see him leave. Also according to some traditions, he avenged his son's death by killing Elena, when the woman returned to Sparta with her husband Menelaus. Teti was also involved in some other divine events: with his sister Eurinome, he welcomed the little Hephaestus lovingly in the waters of the sea, when this god was rejected by his mother Hera and flung down from Olympus. Once grown, to thank her, the divine smith created magnificent jewels for Teti and her sister. When on one occasion He saw them on the blacks, he envied them and asked what a talented goldsmith had created them. Before the queen of the gods, Thetis was forced to reveal that the author of these works was none other than Hephaestus, the son of Hera himself rejected. So Hera requested Teti to inform Hephaestus that she wanted to see him again.

- Toe.

Oceanine

The Oceanines were daughters of the Titan Oceanus and Titanide Thetis, sisters of the three thousand rivers; they were powerful goddesses of the waters and the seas, personifying the running waters, that is, every sea current or great river. They were imagined as beautiful and flourishing girls and represented in the act of dancing, getting wet, or drawing water. At the Oceanines, like the other nymphs, goats were sacrificed and offered oil, honey and focaccia. In Theogony Hesiod it says clearly that the Oceanines are three thousand, but it enumerates only 41. The list below shows all the names provided by Hesiod:

- Acaste.
- Admete.
- Anfiro.
- Asia - He had married the Titan Iapetus, giving him the sons, also often considered to be part of the Titans: Atlas, Prometheus, Epimetheus and Menezio. According to other versions, however, bride of Iapetus and mother of the four Titans would have been another of the Oceanines, Climene.
- Calypso - According to the story of Homer's Odyssey Calypso was instead the daughter of Atlas.
- On his genealogy the sources are divided:
  - Some consider her daughter of Atlas and Pleione: the legend accepted by Homer.
  - Daughter of Elio (the Sun) and of Perseide, then sister of Eete and Circe.
  - According to Hesiod, he was one of the Oceanines, daughters of the Titan Oceano and Titanide Teti.
  - Finally, it appears also in the list of Nereids, the daughters of Nereus and Doris.
- According to the story of the Odyssey of Homer it was, instead, daughter of Atlas and lived on the island of Ogigia, which the authors place in the Mediterranean

West and which is similar to the peninsula of Ceuta, in front of Gibraltar but also a cave on the shore at the sea, on the island of Gozo, it is referred to as the home of Calypso. One day Ulysses, escaped from the vortex of Charybdis, landed on the island and Calypso fell in love with it. The Odyssey tells how she loved him and kept him with her, according to Homer, for seven years (according to Pseudo-Apollodoro five and only one according to Igino) offering him in vain immortality, which the hero insistently refused. Ulysses kept in his heart the desire to return to Ithaca, and did not allow himself to be seduced. Calypso lived in a deep cave, with many rooms, which opened onto natural gardens, a sacred wood with large trees and springs that flowed through the grass. She spent her time spinning, weaving, with the slaves, also nymphs, who sang while they worked. The tears of Ulysses were welcomed by Athena, who, sorry for her protégé, asked Zeus to intervene. The god then sent Hermes to convince Calypso to let him leave and she reluctantly consented. He gave them timber to build a raft, and provisions for the journey. He also indicated to him on which stars to adjust the navigation. The legends after the Odyssey ascribe to Ulisse and Calypso a son, called Latino, more often considered as the son of Circe; sometimes it is said that they had two sons, Nausitoo and Nausinoo, whose names remind the ship. Finally, Ausone, the eponym of Ausonia, is attributed to him as a son.

- Calliroe - From the Greek Kallirroé which means "beautiful flowing water", he joined in marriage with Crisaore the giant armed with a golden sword coming from the head of Medusa, together with the winged horse Pegasus, when Perseus beheaded his head. From the union with Crisaore Gerione was born, a monster with three heads, three bodies and six arms, brother of Echidna. He was a very strong giant with three heads, three busts and only two legs, owner of a kingdom extended to the borders of the mythical Tartessus. He possessed beautiful oxen and Euristeus ordered

Heracles to capture them. Heracles departed and saw the golden boat of Helios and borrowed it. He arrived on the island of Gerion and killed the monster and took the oxen. She was angry, sent a swarm of flies to kill the oxen but Eracle also faced them and won.

- Cercei.
- Climene - He married the Titan Giapeto from whom he generated four sons: Prometheus, Epimetheus, Atlas and Menezio.
- According to other versions, bride of Iapetus and mother of the four Titans her children would have been another of the Oceanines, Asia. According to another version, Climene was not the mother of Prometheus, but his wife, and it was he who made her pregnant with Ellen, the progenitor of the Ellenians, and of Deucalion, husband of Pirra. Or, according to a variant of the myth, Climene instead married Elio, from whom he had Fetonte and the Eliadi. Another bride of Elio would also have been Perseide, another of the Oceanines.
- Clitia.
- Criseide.
- Dione - Its origin varies according to the traditions: according to Apollodorus it is a Titanide, daughter of Uranus (Heaven) and of Gea (the Earth), then sister of Temi, Rea, Teti, Febe, Mnemosine and Teia; according to the version of Hesiod, reported in Theogony, it is one of the Oceanines, and daughter of the titan Oceano and Titanide Teti. Igino, in his Fabulae, instead considers her one of the Pleiades, the daughters of Atlas and Pleione; in this last version, married to Tantalo, he had two sons: Niobe and Pelope. Homer relates that Zeus had married her and had had a daughter, Aphrodite; this legend was also accepted by the poet Virgilio, who names the goddess with the epithet of "Dionea". According to Plato, there were two Aphrodites: the first, born of Uranus, was Aphrodite Urania, goddess of pure love, the second, Aphrodite Pandemia (ie Aphrodite of the People), daughter of Zeus and Dione, goddess of

'vulgar love. Yet this is a late philosophical interpretation, unrelated to the goddess's earliest myths. Dione is also the goddess of the oak, and as such is assimilated to Dionysus, whose mother is often considered the next fruit of her love with Zeus.

- Dori - means the source that benefits man.
- Elettra - Its name indicates the water gushing. Electra with Taumante, son of Ponto, created Iris (personification of the rainbow) and the three Harpies:
  1. Aello - His name meant "swift as the whirlwind". Aello was used by the gods to impose peace and assign the right punishments for the crimes committed. It was initially described as a beautiful winged girl. Later other writers described her as a winged monster with the face of a horrible hag, sometimes half a woman half bird with pointed and curved claws. It is also described as capturing people to lead them to Hades and torturing them.
  2. Ocipete - Its name meant "the fast flowing one".
  3. Celeno - His name meant darkness. Sometimes it was also called Podarge (from the agile foot). According to legend it was Zephyr's lover, the wind that comes from the West, and together with him he generated Balio and Xanto, the two talking horses of Achilles.

The Harpies are monstrous creatures, with a woman's face and a bird's body. The origin of their myth must perhaps be attributed to a personification of the storm. They have sharp claws. It was said that they lived in the Strofadi islands, in the Aegean Sea. Later, Virgil places them in the antechamber of the Underworld, with the other monsters. The legend in which they perform the most important function is that concerning the plague of Fineo, the Thracian king who gave hospitality to the Argonauts during their journey to Colchis. Flitting in the room where Fineo feasted, the Harpies took possession of his food and soiled his table with their droppings. Fineo made an agreement with the Argonauts allowing them to prophesy their future if they had freed them from that scourge. Calaide and Zete, the winged sons of Borea, rose with the sword in their hands and pursued the Harpies to the Strofadi islands in the Aegean Sea where Iris intervened and promised that the Harpies would return to their cave on Mount Ditte in Crete and never again molested Fineo. According to another tradition pursuers and pursued they never did return and died of hunger and the river Arpis (the Tigris), in the Peloponnese, got this name because one of them trying to escape from Calaide and Zete drowned in its depths. Aeneas met the Celian harpy at the Strofades where he predicted that his Trojans would reach the new land only when hunger drove them to even eat the tables. Together with his companions he took possession of the Trojans' food and since their steel feathers were harder than swords, it was impossible to drive them away. Elettra was a nymph who was consecrated amber, an important material for those who traveled in the sea at that time.

- According to Homer, Electra and Zeus conceived Dardanus, the forefather of the kings of Troy, and therefore called Dardanides.
- Eudore - means the source that gives good gifts to man.
- Eurynome - It would have been the third wife of Zeus, with whom he would have generated the Carites.
- Europe.
- Galaxaure - Means the source of white water as milk.
- Ianira.
- Iante - Its name indicates the violet color.
- Idua - She was the youngest of them all, she married King Eete of Colchis and procured Calciope and Medea.
- Calciope, also called Iofossa, joined Frisso, the character who arrived in Colchis flying on the back of a ram with a golden fleece. Medea, daughter of Eete, king of Colchis, and of Idua, was also nephew of Elio (according to other sources of Apollo) and of the sorceress Circe, and how the latter was endowed with

magical powers. Instead, according to the variation of the myth (Diodoro Siculo), the sun, Elio, had two sons, Perse and Eeta. She lost a daughter, Hecate, a very powerful sorceress, who killed him and later joined her uncle Eeta. Circe, Medea and Egialpo were born from this union. Medea is one of the most famous and controversial characters in Greek mythology. Its name in Greek means "tricks, screeds", in fact, the tradition describes it as a witch with powers even divine. When Jason arrives in Colchis together with the Argonauts in search of the Golden Fleece, capable of healing the wounds, guarded by a fierce and terrible dragon on behalf of Eete, she falls madly in love. And, just to help him achieve his goal, he comes to kill his brother Apsirto, spreading the poor remains behind him after having embarked on the ship Argo along with Jason, who became her husband. The father, thus, being forced to pick up his son's limbs, can not reach the expedition, and the Argonauts return to Iolco with the Golden Fleece. The uncle of Jason, Pelias, refuses, however, to grant the throne to his nephew, as he had previously promised, in exchange for the Vello: Medea then exploits their magical abilities and with the deception becomes the protagonist of new heights to help the beloved . Convince, in fact, the daughters of Pelia to give the father a "pharmakòn", after having broken it up and boiled, which would have completely rejuvenated: proves the validity of his art by bringing a goat to the condition of lamb, after chopped and boiled with magical herbs. The naive daughters are deceived and thus cause the death of the father, amid atrocious suffering: Acasto, son of Pelia, pitifully buries those poor remains and banishes Medea and Jason from Iolco, forcing them to take refuge in Corinth, where they will get married.

- Ippo.
- Melobosi - means the source where the flocks are watered.
- Menesto.

- Metes - She was the mother of the powerful goddess Athena.
- His name means "prudence" but also "perfidy". It was she who saved the master of lightning from his father's Chrono. In fact, it had been predicted that one of the sons would have dethroned him by killing him, so that, to be sure, he devoured his offspring alive. Meti handed a drug to the titan who vomited all his children. It is opposed to the Ananke, to fatality. According to the myth was also the first lover (and perhaps the first wife) of Zeus, the father of all gods, but the woman did not easily surrender to the god, turning into a thousand ways trying to escape him, before surrendering. Another oracle had predicted that Zeus would be dethroned by a son he had from Meti and then after having lain with her, he decided to devour her. Zeus then led her to turn into a drop of water, (in Greek mythology, intelligence and cunning were represented as poliforms and in constant change: Meti, in fact, is able to assume any form of desire) and incorporated it drinking it . According to another version, it was transformed into a cicada or a fly and swallowed up by Zeus, who claimed that he sometimes heard the voice of Meti giving him suggestions. At this point a powerful headache came to the god, and thanks to the help of Hephaestus or Prometheus, the immortal skull of Zeus was smashed with an ax and Athena emerged from the wound.
- Ociroe - United to the god Elio gave him a son, called Fasi.
- Pasitoe.
- Peito.
- Perseid - He was the wife of Elio, and he had many children:
  - Eete, king of the city of Eea sul Fasi, in Colchis.
  - Pasifae, wife of Minos, queen of Crete and mother of the Minotaur.
  - Circe, the sorcerer who tricked Ulysses.

- Circe lived on the island of Eea and was the daughter of Elio and the nymph Perseide and sister of Eete (king of Colchis) and of Pasifae (wife of Minos), as well as aunt of Medea. According to another tradition, she is a daughter of Day and Night. According to what Euripides reports in Medea, the latter is described as a daughter of the sovereigns of Colchis, or Eete and Hecate. Being Eete son of the Sun, then Circe would be sister of the king and aunt of Medea. Eete's etymology would also explain the etymology of the island where Circe, Eea, lives. Ulysses, after visiting the village of Lestrigoni, going up the Italian coast, reaches the island of Eea. The island, covered by dense vegetation, seems uninhabited and Ulysses sends a part of his crew to the reconnaissance, under the guidance of Euryloco. In a valley the men discover that outside a palace, from which a melodious voice resounds, there are ferocious animals. All men, with the exception of Euryloco, enter the palace and are welcomed by the owner, who is nothing but the sorceress Circe. Men are invited to participate in a banquet but, as soon as they taste the food, they are turned into pigs (or pigs are said to have given birth), lions, dogs, depending on their character and their nature. Soon after, Circe pushes them towards the stables and closes them up. Euryloco quickly returns to the ship and tells Ulysses what happened. The ruler of Ithaca decides to go to the sorceress to try to save his companions. Heading towards the palace, he meets the god Hermes, messenger of the gods, who reveals the secret to remain immune to Circe's spells. If he mixes in what Circe offers him to drink a magic herb called moly, he will not undergo any transformation. Ulysses reaches the sorceress, who offers him to drink (as he had done with his companions), but Ulysses, having had the precaution of mixing the moly with the drink, does not turn into an animal. He threatens to kill Circe, who recognizes his own defeat and restores human companions to Ulysses even to all the others turned into wild beasts. Ulysses spends with her a year and has a son, Telegono, and perhaps a daughter, called Cassifone. An appendix of Hesiod's Theogony tells that their sons are two: Anzio and Latino, who reigned over the Tirreni. Ulysses is forced to yield to the wishes of his companions, who want to return home, and asks Circe the best way to return. The sorceress advised him to visit the underworld and to consult the shadow of the Tiresias, then Ulysses leaves with his ship. In the end, no longer driven by curiosity as in the cave of Polyphemus, but by the duty to save his companions, Ulysses manages to calm the waters again. These, however, will be the cause of so much suffering for him, because by using them, the god Poseidon will make the return (in Greek Nostos) of the hero to Ithaca, by his beloved and faithful wife Penelope, ever more tortuous.

- Petrea - means the source of the rocks.
- Pleaxure - means the source from the gush that cuts through the air.
- Pluto.
- Polidore - means the source that gives many gifts to man.
- Primno.
- Rodeia - Its name indicates the source of the roses.
- Stige - It was the most illustrious and powerful of the Oceanines.
- Stige was the goddess of the river of the same name, the Styx, on which the Olympian gods performed their oaths, drinking the waters. According to Ovid's Metamorphosis, it was the oldest of the Oceanines and also Hesiod recognized it as "the most illustrious" among them; it is the only one that presides over a river, the infernal Stige, whose task it is to guard the waters. Joining the titan Pallante he generated Nike (Victory), Zelos (the ardor), Bia (the Force) and Cratos (the Power). Although belonging to the lineage of the Titans, Stige allied himself with Zeus and the Olympians in their war against those primordial deities,

helping his mighty sons to join what would later become the king of the Gods. To thank her later Zeus rewarded her with a great honor: the gods would have sworn the truth about her waters, drinking them. If the god affirmed the truth, he would not have suffered any consequences, but if he swore the forgery, he would have been struck by a sort of painful "stupor" that would have paralyzed him for a while. The waters of Styx, on the other hand, were deadly if drunk by ordinary men. According to a tradition, Stige has created together with her lover Zeus, the goddess of the underworld Persephone. Their amorous and procreative relationship occurred after the defeat of the Titans, during the Titanomachia. The sty-nymphs are also protagonists in the myth of Perseus, as they kept the objects necessary for the hero to carry out his business; but since they were invisible and unobtainable, Perseus had to get information about them at the Graia to reach them.

- Telesto.
- Toe.
- Tyche.
- Urania.
- Xante.
- Zeuxo.

Pleiades

The Pleiades, named by the Romans Vergilie, were born on Mount Cillene. Pleiades means "doves", or, according to another theory, the term is related to the verb plei (navigate), because the stars appear in the sky at the most opportune moments for sailors. They were seven sisters, daughters of Atlas and Pleione, but for some they were daughters of a queen of the Amazons.

Atlas - He was a titan son of Iapetus and of Climene.
But according to a more curious version, he would be the son of Zeus and of Climene, while according to Plato he would be the son of Poseidon and Clitus. According to Hesiod, Zeus forced him to keep the entire heavenly vault over his shoulders. The punishment was inflicted on him for allied with the father of Zeus, Cronus, who led the revolt against the gods of Olympus. In the Odyssey (book I) it is described poetically as one of the pillars of the sky. Still in the Odyssey, he is referred to as the father of Calypso. Atlas managed to convince Heracles to temporarily replace him in his punishment, provided he went to collect the golden apples of the Hesperides. However, it was very difficult for Heracles to convince Atlante to resume his post, and he had to resort to a stratagem. Atlas created the Pleiades, the Iadi, the Iante, the Esperidi and Calypso. According to a tradition, the titan was petrified by Perseus who showed him the head of Medusa to punish him for not hosting him and so Atlas became the mountain chain of the same name in the north of Africa. The first vertebra of the vertebral column, atlas, owes its name to this character, since it supports the skull as the titan holds the celestial sphere.

Pleione - She was a little sister; he married Atlante and, in love with him, had the Pleiades. According to one of the versions, the Pleiades were the virgin companions of Artemis, the Goddess of Hunting. Orion, the famous hunter, chased them all over the earth and they fled to the fields of Boeotia. The Gods moved compassionately, turning the girls into doves and then immortalizing their figure in the stars. Yet none of the Pleiades was a virgin, almost all lay with gods, except Merope, married to the notorious criminal Sisyphus, who for the shame abandoned his sisters in heaven and, for this reason, it is said that Merope shines in the sky less than the other stars that they form the Pleiades. Once they became stars, thanks also to the powers of Zeus, they showed their sympathy to Atreus, modifying their course. According to another version of the myth, they were kidnapped by an Egyptian and freed by the brave Heracles. Finally, according to a further version, after the death of their sisters, the Iadi, they killed themselves. In all versions, however, the fate of the Pleiades is always to become stars.

The names of the Pleiades were:

- Alcyone - Alcione elected to command the seven Pleiades, led the fishermen with their sisters, once they became stars. When they started, the most favorable period for anyone who wanted to fish began while at the sunset, an icy wind blew. For this reason, the Aeolians define Alcione as a goddess and venerated her as such, to whom they prayed to foster the winds and avoid the shoals. According to Pausanias he had two sons from Poseidon: Anthas and Iperete. Anthas, a Greek hero, founded according to tradition many cities including Alicarnasso, a city in which he transferred the cult of Poseidon "Phytalmios". From Anthas the descendants of the Anteados were born, priests involved in this cult, which was forbidden to eat fish. Anthas had a brother, Iperete, also a famous builder who often helped him to build cities, like Antheia and Hypereia, which later joined in giving life to the city of Trezene in Argolis, so called by Pitteo. He had a son, Ezio, who did not give his father great honor.

- Celeno - He married Poseidon and was made into his mother by Lico, Nitteo, Euripilo and, perhaps, Tritone. Lico is a figure from Greek mythology, son of Poseidon. He was exiled with his brother Nittao for the killing of Flegia, the son of Ares. They settled in Tebe, where Lico became king and married Dirce. As a king he welcomed his niece Antiope, expelled by Nittao, but treated her like a slave. When Antiope gave birth to twins, Amphion and Zeto, Lico ordered them to abandon them on Mount Citerone, so that they would die. The newborns were found by chance by a shepherd, who raised them as children. Meanwhile, Lico's wife, Dirce, treated Antiope even more cruelly, forcing her to flee. He found refuge with the abandoned children who, having become adults, avenged their mother, killing Lico and dragging Dirce from an ox. The twins took possession of the Theban realm and built a new city at the foot of Cadmea. Another myth states that Lico was killed by Heracles, having raped his wife, Megara, that Heracles would then kill in a fit of madness. According to some legends, Celeno was also the mother of Deucalione, who was given by Prometheus.

- Elettra - Elettra used to live in the island of Samothrace. Electra, along with two of her sisters, was loved by Zeus; from their union was born Dardano, the forefather of the Troia dynasty, who abandoned the land where the Pleiades had given birth to him to go to Troas. The second son he had from Zeus was Iasion, who as an adult was a lover of the goddess Demeter. Finally he also had a daughter, Armonia whom the father of the gods assigned as a bride to the hero Cadmus. Sometimes it was attributed to her a fourth child that she would always have had from Zeus, Emazione, who, unlike her brothers, remained in Samothrace and here reigned there until her death. The legend of Elettra also connected to the sacred Palladio. Zeus, struck by a violent love for her, wanted to rape her but the girl fled and sought refuge by throwing herself at the precious simulacrum. However, it did not help because Zeus succeeded in his intent and made the young woman pregnant. Fallen vaginal blood, a sign of lost virginity, fell on the statue, profaning it. Angered, the goddess Athena, owner of the simulacrum, threw the Palladium and the same Elettra on earth. Or it was Zeus himself, angry about Elettra's opposition, who threw her indignantly on the ground. According to other legends, it was Elettra who gave the sacred statue to her son Dardano, who placed it inside the city he founded as a protection for the entire fortress. At the end of the Trojan war, Elettra, who had witnessed from heaven to all the deeds of her illustrious son's descendants, was consumed with grief at the sight of the mythical city of Troy in flames. In despair she was transformed, together with her sisters, into a star, in the current constellation of the Pleiades.

- Maia - Ermes was born from his union with Zeus.
  Hermes plays the role of messenger of the gods. Son of Zeus and Piaiade Maia, he is one of the twelve gods Olimpi. His symbols were the rooster and the turtle but he was clearly recognizable also for his purse, his winged sandals and hat and the messenger's stick, the kerykeion. In Roman mythology the correspondent of Hermes was Mercury who, although he was a god of Etruscan origin, possessed many characteristics similar to him, as being the god of commerce. Temples dedicated to Hermes were widespread throughout Greece, but the most important center where his cult was practiced was Feneo in Arcadia where the celebrations in his honor were held called "Hermoea". The god Hermes played the role of psychopomp, that is, accompanying the spirit of the dead, which helps to find the way to the underworld of the afterlife, and is one of the few who can attend the underworld. In the Homeric hymn to Demeter, Hermes reports Persephone sound and saved by his mother Demeter. Hermes accompanies the souls of Penelope's suitors killed by Odysseus in the

underworld. Hermes helped Perseus kill the gorgon Medusa by giving him his winged sandals and the sickle of Zeus. He also gave Perseus the helmet of Hades that had the power to make invisible, advising him to use it to avoid being seen by the immortal sisters of Medusa. Athena also provided her help to Perseus, lending him his shining shield. It is said that Maia, symbol of spring or of the fertile rainy season (someone says that the month of May, in Latin Maius, derives from this name) was the most beautiful of the Pleiades and that, together with the sisters, was transformed into a star from Zeus to steal it from his jealous wife.

- Merope - The girl married Sisyphus, king of Corinth (called Efira at that time), from whom he had Glaucus as a son, father of Bellerophon. Ovid indicates it as the least bright star in the constellation of the Pleiades, as the only one to have married a mortal.

- Sterope - Her figure is linked to that of Enomao who according to some myths was her husband and according to others her son, generated by the union with Ares. Enomao was the king of Pisa, promoter of the first race that took place from the parts of Olimpia. This consisted of a bet against anyone who wanted to marry Hippodamia's daughter, to avoid her marriage: he challenged the pretenders to a four-legged race, whose route went from his palace to the altar of Poseidon on the isthmus of Corinth. If the rival had won he would have become a spouse of his daughter, but if he had lost, Oenomaus would have killed him. The king was the son of the god Ares, who had given him a draft of rapids as fast as the wind, and his chariot was led by Mirtylus, son of Hermes, the most expert of the charioteers. In addition, the tyrant took a further guarantee, demanding that Hippodamia ascended the pretender's chariot, so that he, absorbed in the contemplation of the beautiful girl, would lose the necessary concentration. Enomao, sure however of his success, granted an advantage to his rival. When he had left, he sacrificed a ram to Zeus and, only after the end of the sacrifice, he began to chase him. Inevitably the adversary lost, and the king pierced him with his spear and cut off his head, which he nailed to his palace. Thirteen heads already, when a new young champion presented himself to the challenge: Pelops. Hippodamia fell in love with the young man at first sight, and persuaded Mirtilo - who was in love with her - to tamper with the wheels of his father's wagon, so as to make him lose.Pausania, however, tells us that it was Pelope himself to deal with Mirtilo, promising him half of the kingdom and the ius primae noctis with Hippodamia, promises that both renounced at the end of the race. In both versions, however, during the race, Enomao's chariot was destroyed, and he became entangled in the reins and was swept to the ground. On his deathbed he understood the betrayal of his charioteer, and cursed him, wishing him to be killed by Pelops himself. The ominous prediction inevitably came to fruition when Mirtilo, not having forgotten his love for Hippodamia (or the promise of Pelops), tried to rape her, on the road to Cape Geresto, the southernmost point of the Evia. Pelops, aware of the thing, hurled Mirtilo with a kick in the sea that took from him the name of Mirtoo. We also learn from Igino, in his Astronomy that his father Hermes gave his son a celestial seat, turning it into the constellation dell'auriga.

- Taigete - He tried to escape Zeus, who wanted to covet it, invoking Artemis who turned her into a fawn. Returning to the human form, Taigete consecrated the Cerva deer to the huntress goddess. According to other myths Zeus still managed to join her, and Lacedemone was born from them. Lacedemon was king of Laconia and according to tradition he founded the city of Sparta, called Lacedemone, and first introduced the cult of Graces in Greece. He married Sparta, daughter of

Eurotas, from whom he had a son, Amicla, and a daughter, Eurydice.

Hyades

The Iadi were nymphs of the woods, the sources and the marshes, in fact their name means "rainy".
The myths bring us the seven names of these nymphs:
- Ambrosia
- Eudora
- Pasitoe
- Coronide
- Polisso
- Fileto
- Dione

They were daughters of Atlas and Etra, as well as sisters of Iante and the Pleiades. Some myths tell of their participation in the education of Dionysus. From Zeus they were turned into stars, Iadi, and placed in front of the constellation of Taurus. However it seems that the name of the cluster derives from the ancient Egyptian: already in the texts of the pyramids we find, in fact, a word, iad, written with the determinative of the star, which has the general sense of influence, influence and even pestilence.
Another word, iadt, is also translated with torrential rains. From the commentary to the Pap. Smith by J.H. Breasted then know that iadt was an annual disease. There is also a word iadj, with similar meanings, but written with the determinative that indicates the city and the being.
Now the connection between the Egyptian name (iad, iadj, iadt) and the cluster in discourse is clear, since from the highest antiquity the appearance of these stars marked the beginning of the rains.

Eliadi

The Eliadi were the nymphs daughters of the Sun (Apollo) and of the little ocean Climene and they were the sisters of Fetonte.
According to the myth, Fetonte, to show Epafo that Apollo was really his father, begged him to let him drive the chariot of the Sun; but, because of his inexperience, he lost control of it, the horses went wild and ran wildly for the celestial vault: first they climbed too high, burning a stretch of the sky that became the Milky Way, then they went down too close to the earth, devastating Libya that became a desert.
The inhabitants of the earth asked for help from Zeus who intervened to save the earth and, angry, threw a thunderbolt at Fetonte, who fell at the mouth of the river Eridano (the Po), perhaps in today's Barberry or in the lands of Alfonsine. Her sisters, the Eliadi, frightened, cried abundant tears with a plagued face and were transformed by the gods into white poplars.
Their tears became amber. Another version tells, instead, that Fetonte precipitated in the thermal area of the Euganean Hills, between Abano Terme and Montegrotto, connecting with the local cult of the Venetian god Aponus, identified with Apollo. In fact, according to an ancient legend, the Popes, which we usually find grouped together three by three, were once part of the Eliadi family.
Their names and their number varies according to the authors, among them we can mention:
- Astride
- Dioxippe
- Egle
- Elie
- Febe
- Fetusa
- Lamezia

According to another myth, Eliadi were the seven sons of the nymph Rodhos. They were revered as patrons of navigation and considered the inventors of the seasons and those who divided time in days and hours; they also became famous astronomers.

Hesperides

The Hesperides are figures from Greek mythology, daughters of the Night. According to the legends, they guarded the garden of Hera's golden apples, fruits that gave immortality. Later versions make her daughters of Atlas. The Hesperides were nymphs whose genealogy often remains confused: they are sometimes named as daughters of the Night, of Teti and Oceano, of Zeus and Temi, of Forco and Ceto and also, according to the most accredited theory, of Atlas and Hesperides. Their number is also uncertain, so much so that some mythographers name five Hesperides, others name seven. On the other hand, those who underline that there were three, connect them to the triple goddess of the Moon in her appearance as a sovereign of death:

- Egle
- Erizia
- Esperaretusa

It remains certain that they lived in the extreme West of the world, beyond the confines of the inhabited earth, and there they had a wonderful garden where they had the task of guarding the precious tree that gave gold apples, gift of Gaea for the wedding of Zeus with Hera . For greater security, so that the same Hesperides did not catch the prodigious apples, Hera had ordered the snake Ladone of the hundred heads to preside over the guard, being constantly rolled around the trunk of the tree. King Eurystheus heard about these fruits and commanded Hercules to bring them to him, so the hero after the undertaking of the red oxen immediately set off in search of the garden of the Hesperides. During his wanderings, one day he stopped on the banks of a lake to rest and from the waters of the lake emerged a nymph who asked Hercules the reason for his exhaustion; the hero explained to the nymph that he was looking for the garden of the Hesperides and the nymph advised him to turn to Nereus. Nereus, who was a deity of the sea that could take any form, to escape the question of Hercules began to assume all possible and imaginable forms to scare him, but accustomed to much worse Hercules remained there to wait for the end of the show; so Nereo, demonstrating the courage of the young man, told Hercules that the garden of the Hesperides was in Mauritania, the country where the Titan Atlas, the father of the Hesperides, was king.

When he reached the extreme western hemisphere of the world, where he found Atlas supporting the heavy vault of the sky over his shoulder, the hero proudly presented him with the desire to have the golden fruit of his garden; Atlante consented, however, making him notice that the fruits could catch only him and that he had a problem: who would have supported the sky in his place? Hercules immediately proposed himself as his substitute. Atlas went to gather the fruits; returning, however, he told Hercules that he did not feel like resuming the awkward task of supporting such a burden on his shoulders since he had found such a good substitute. As for the fruit of gold, he would have brought them to Euristeo himself.

Hercules pretended to agree with the solution and asked a favor to Atlas, to replace him for a moment in order to change his back; Atlas fell into the trap and Hercules managed to escape with the booty. It is said, on the other hand, that Heracles killed the snake by shooting an arrow above the garden walls built by Atlas.

He could only ease his grief over the death of Ladon by placing his image between the stars, as a constellation of the Serpent; the apples captured by Heracles were then returned to them by Euristeus. According to other sources, the pomes returned to Heracles instead; these, in turn, gave them to Aphrodite or to Athena: the goddess finally decided to make them to Hera, since it was not correct that they were given to anyone. There is, however, a sad conclusion: the day after the accomplishment of Heracles' enterprise, in the same garden the Argonauts arrived, who witnessed the transformation into trees of the Hesperides (a black poplar, a willow and an elm), desperate death. for the loss of their treasure and their beloved guardian-protector.

The golden knobs of the Hesperides also appear in the myth of Atalanta, a very fast girl in the race who challenged her suitors by putting herself as a prize.

One of these suitors was Melanione (or Hippomenes) who, asking for help from Aphrodite, received from the goddess three golden apples from the Garden of the Hesperides, which in turn Heracles had given her. While the race was taking place, Ippomene tossed the knobs one after the other on the ground, so that Atalanta, irresistibly attracted, stopped to pick them up, losing the contest.

Night

Night or Nyx is one of the primordial deities of Greek mythology. According to Hesiod's Theogony, Night was the daughter of Chaos, while in Orphic cosmogony she was the daughter of Phanes; in the Fabulae, Igino Astronomo tells her daughter of Chaos and of Caligine. According to Hesiod, Night was the personification of the terrestrial night, as opposed to his brother Erebus, who represented the night of the infernal world. It was also opposed to his sons Etere (the light) and Emera (the day). Night was one of the most ancient deities, and dwelt in Hades; according to Homer, Zeus was also afraid of it. Night was the mother of some of the other primordial deities: according to Hesiod (Teogonia) and Cicero (De natura deorum), his brother Erebus Notte had Etere and Emera; according to Cicero and Igino he was also mother of Eros, always from Erebo; Bacchilide says instead that Emera conceived it with Crono. Besides these children, she is also credited with the motherhood of many other figures in Greek mythology, mostly daimones (sometimes called "personifications").

Erebus, ancestral deity, son of Chaos and brother of the Night, is the personification of darkness, and with the term "Erebus", in fact, we can also indicate the Underworld. With his sister he generated Emera (personification of the day) and Ether (personification of the highest sky, where there is pure light), Ipno (god of sleep) and also Charon. Besides these, Erebo also generated the three Moires with the Night. According to ancient philosophers, this myth symbolizes the manifestation of the cosmos starting from chaos or unmanifest essence.

Emera is the personification of the Day.
He has a brother named Etere, of whom he was a wife and with whom he would have a daughter, Talassa. According to other mythographers his father was Elio, while in some poems among the sons of Emera and Aether also figure Uranus.

Ether is the divine power of the higher and purer sky, of the brightness of the day. It is the divinity of the upper air that only the gods breathe, as opposed to the air breathed by mortals. Igino, Latin-American mythographer of the II century AD, in the Fabulae writes that he was the son of Caligine (Dark) and Chaos. Da Giorno (Dies) had as its children the Earth and the Sky (Caelum) and the Sea. While his daughter Terra had descent: Pain (Dolor), Deception (Dolus), Ira, Lutto (Luctus), Menzogna (Mendacium), Oath (Iusiurandum), Vendetta (Ultio), Intemperanza (Intemperantia), Disputa (Altercatio), Forgetfulness (Obliuio), Dullness (Socordia), Fear (Timor), Superbiation, Incestum (Incestum), Battle (Pugna), Ocean (Oceanus), Themis, Tartarus (Tartarus), Ponto (Pontus), Titans (Titanes) and the three Furies (Furiae).

Apate

Apate was the divinity of deception, she was one of the spirits in Pandora's box. His parents were Nyx and Erebo.
In Mineralogy from its name comes Apatite which is calcium fluorophosphate. This mineral takes its name because it "deceives" by being confused by external characteristics with other minerals. In fact, Apatite presents itself with different colors, it is also remembered that the basic building block of the human bone structure is made of hydroxyapatite crystals.
In the Greek myth among the various stories handed down on the betrayals of Zeus to his wife Hera there is that of the relationship between Zeus and Semele for which Hera, furious at yet another betrayal of the Olympic husband, turns to Apate, who lends her a surrounded by that worn by Aphrodite who was able to make lying to the listener seem true. He was directing his steps to Thebes, adorned with this girdle, under the aspect of the old nurse of Cadmus. She was, thus disguised, advises Semele to ask Zeus for proof of her identity as the god of his love for her; at this point Semele is prey to the jealousy that dwells in Hera and wants to join Zeus when the god has his "true" appearance and not misrepresented as he does with all his other mortal lovers. But love with a god is a fire and as such burns it while Hermes saves the immature fetus, the fruit of the embrace, from the stake. The saved fetus will then be Dionysus. Semele will then be welcomed into Olympus under the name of Tione, as revenge has appeased Era.

Eris

Eris is a figure of Greek mythology, she is a minor goddess, to be precise "the goddess of discord".
It is linked to Ares, which often accompanies it, and according to some it guarded the palace of the god of war, in Thrace. The most significant episode to which the goddess is linked is that of the apple of discord: furious at the exclusion from Peleus and Teti's wedding banquet, Eris even came to contemplate the idea of hurling the Titans against the other Olympians, who had been all invited, and dethrone Zeus. Then, however, he chose a more subtle way to carry out his revenge. When she reached the place where the banquet was held, she rolled a golden apple, according to some taken in the garden of the Hesperides, declaring that it was destined "to the most beautiful" among the divine guests. The dispute that arose between Hera, Athena and Aphrodite for the allocation of the fruit and the relative title, led to the judgment of Paris and following the rape of Helen who originated the war of Troy. Initially the choice was up to Zeus, but he did not want to choose, because it would unleash the ire of the "losers" goddesses forever. He therefore decided to entrust the task to a mortal. He chose Paris, because, as past events had witnessed, the young man was skilled and just in judging.
Despite being a deity, the role of Eris in Greek mythology is marginal, limited mostly to short appearances on the battlefields, especially during the Trojan War. The goddess is often specially sent by Zeus to arouse the spirits of the combatants with his shouts: not only those of the Greeks, for whom he sided like Ares, but also those of the Trojans. His fury, however, exceeds that of his brother, to the point that Eris often remains to rejoice in the blood shed by men even after the other gods have withdrawn, and loves to walk among the bodies of the dead and dying when the clash has already ended . We know that she forged the halberd with which the rider Penthesilea, daughter of Ares, fought in the war of Troy, and who appeared in Dionysus' dream, under the disguise of Rhea, to reproach the

god for his idlings and urge him to resume the battle with the king of India, enticing him with the prefiguration of his upcoming ascent to Olympus.

He helped Hephaestus to forge the necklace of Harmony, which played its disastrous role in the events of the Seven against Thebes and their Epigones. Eris also played a role in the affair of the Golden Fleece, at the time when this had taken possession of Tieste, allowing him to become king of Mycenae, to the detriment of the other pretender to the throne, Atreus.

Zeus, who favored the latter, obtained from Tieste the promise that he would give up the throne if the sun had changed its course. Then, the god sent Eris on the path of Elio's cart, and the goddess set the path of the evening under the hooves of the dawn horse, so that the sun that day, halfway through the celestial vault, reversed its normal path and set in the east. Finally, when Politecno and Aedona di Colofone claimed to love each other more than Zeus and Era, the infuriated goddess sent Eris among them to give rise to a dispute, the final outcome of which was the murder of her husband by Aedona.

Geras

Geras was the god of old age.
It was considered a virtue because more gēras a man had, more kleos (fame) and arete (excellence and courage) was considered to have. According to Hesiod, Gēras was the son of Nix. Igino adds that his father was Erebo.
He was depicted as a small wrinkled old man.
The opposite of Geras was Hebe, the goddess of youth.
Its Roman equivalent was Senectus.
His figure is known above all thanks to the representations on the vases that show him with the hero Heracles; unfortunately, the myth that represented it has been completely lost.

Hypnos

Hypnos is the god of sleep, son of Erebo and twin brother of Thanatos. Ipno, according to Homer, lived in Lemno.
Another version is made by the husband of Pasitea, one of the Charites, originally from that city. For Virgilio he lived in the vestibule of Hades, for Ovid in the distant Cimmeri country.
The power of Ipno was such that he could sleep men and gods. In the XIV canto of the Iliad He was asked to put Zeus to sleep, so that Poseidon might bring help to the Greeks without the king of the gods coming to know.
In the fifth book of the Aeneid bathes with a branch soaked in water, the face of the helmsman Palinuro, to doze it and make it fall into the sea. Also to the god belong the Doors of Sleep, in the VI book, at the exit of Hades. He had numerous sons, of which the principal ones are Morpheus, Momo, Icelo, Fobetore and Fantaso.
It was Ipno who gave Endymion the ability to sleep with his eyes open. He is portrayed as a naked young man with wings on his head.

Ker

Ker or Chere was in Greek mythology the personification of the destiny of warriors or of the violent death that struck during duels or furtive actions.

Hesiod in his Theogony, he distinguishes it in two figures (such as Death or Destiny). In verse 211 as Ker, Violent Death, born from Nyx for parthenogenesis, then, in verse 217 is mentioned in plural, the Keres, always daughters of Nyx, to be intended as sent of Destiny. The latter are sometimes identified with the Moire.

They represent either directly the violent Death, or the Destiny that accompanies every human being, marking the vital rhythms and outlining the type of death that will fall to the subject; therefore in dangerous moments like battles and heroic actions, the Chere, in both conceptions, flank the individual.

They are sometimes depicted as winged black creatures with sharp teeth and claws, which feed on the blood of the dead and wounded.

Momo

Momo, the blame, is the son of the Night (Nyx).

Cicero says he is the son of the Night and of Ipno (Hypnos).

He was represented as a small, bald man, without clothes and with a mask and a cane in his hand.

According to Hesiod personified sarcasm and mania to censor.

He was furious when he could not criticize Afrodite in any way.

According to another tradition it was Momo who criticized Zeus when the father of the gods wanted to destroy humanity with lightning and flooding, convincing him instead to favor the marriage of Teti and Peleo, which would lead to the end of the hero kingdom. According to another version, it seems that Zeus has driven him out of Olympus, after Momo had harshly criticized an animal created by the king of the gods.

According to a myth, he was invited by Zeus, Athena and Prometheus to judge who had made the best invention of them; Zeus introduced the bull, Athena the house and Prometheus the man, but Momo thought that everyone lacked something. The bull had the horns placed, not above the eyes, but at the sides of the head, making it more difficult to hit the target. The house was not transportable.
Man lacked a way to see in his heart and in his feelings. Finally, the gods grew tired of his burlesque nature and drove him away from Olympus.
He was depicted as a dwarf, bald, naked and with a mask in his hand. Finding no fault in Aphrodite, he began to say that the goddess's sandals creaked.

Moros

In Greek mythology Moros is the personification of the adverse and inevitable destiny, which brings every being, mortal or less towards its predetermined end.
Very little is known about him, except that he is omnipresent, omniscient and omnipotent, even Zeus can not defeat him.
He is the son of Nix and brother of other deities such as Eris, Thanatos and Hypnos. According to tradition, it was conceived without the need of the male counterpart like his brothers and sisters, but according to Igino, Nix conceived it with Erebo.

Nemesis

Nemesis is a Goddess of the Ancient Greek Religions, according to some daughter of Zeus, according to other daughter of Oceano and Notte and then possessed by the same Zeus in the temple of Ramnunte, from which the egg of Helena was born.

The name derives from the Greek and was the name of the Goddess "Distribution of Justice" (justice as a legal code was instead attributed to the Goddess Diche).

Nemesi above all provided justice to unresolved or unpunished crimes, distributing and spraying joy or pain according to what was right, especially by persecuting the wicked and ungrateful to fate. There is no corresponding Goddess in the Roman Religion, which instead inherited the hour Diche as a Goddess of jurisdiction (the actual Justitia, the one with the eye patch and the balance in hand); however, the Romans dedicated an altar to Nemesis on the Campidoglio, where soldiers used to lay down a sword before leaving for the war.

Nemesis means distribution of Fate, understood as Compensating or Repairing Justice, or also interpreted as Divine Justice. Today this term is also used to understand a negative situation that comes immediately after a particularly fortunate period, always as an act predestined to compensation. The idea underlying this term is of a world that responds to a law of harmony, so that good should be compensated for by evil in equal measure.

Achlys

Achlys in Greek mythology was the goddess of misery and misfortune. She was a daughter of the Night and twin of the god Momo. His Latin name was Miseria instead.

She is also the goddess of poisons, and is depicted sitting on a rock, very thin with tattered clothes.

Her cheeks were soiled with blood, as if she had scratched herself. He holds the shield of Hercules on the ground, where she is represented in that same position.

The legend says that Hercules placed Achlys on his shield, so the last image that his enemies would have had before he died would have been the goddess of Misery.

Thanatos

Tànato or Thánatos was the personification of death, son of the Night (or of Astrèa) for parthenogenesis (or from Erebo), as well as the twin brother of Hypnos, the Sleep. He was a minor deity in Greek mythology, often quoted but rarely represented as a person. He performed the function of an angel of death and when the time given to a mortal expired he came, cut a lock of hair for Hades and took him with him. Thanatos's character as an unavoidable and inflexible power failed in a popular myth already quoted by Homer and developed in the satyr's drama Sisyphus fugitive by Aeschylus, where Zeus to punish Sisyphus, king of Corinth, sent Thanatos to lock him up in Tartarus. But when Thanatos arrived at Sisyphus' house, he got him drunk and bound him with chains, imprisoning him. With Thanatos chained, death disappeared from the world.

The god Ares, when he realized that during the battles no one no longer died and that therefore no longer made sense, he moved to free Thanatos and take Sisyphus. Sisyphus succeeded a second time in escaping death by persuading Persephone to have him return to his wife for a day by claiming that she had never succeeded in giving him an appropriate funeral (in fact he had forced his wife Merope not to bury her body). This second time Sisyphus was dragged into the hereafter, up to Tartarus, by Hermes, when he refused to accept his own death; in addition it was condemned for eternity to drag, on top of a hill, a boulder that would then roll down.

If Sisyphus was the only one who could escape the inexorable Thanatos thanks to the deception, Heracles was the only one who could escape thanks to his strength, as Euripides staged in the tragedy Alcestis. Thanatos was often represented as a child often winged and in company with his brother Hypnos, with a Torchia turned as a symbol of life that dies out, or with a butterfly in hand or with a poppy flower sleeping pill, a symbol that shared with his brother. If portrayed as an adult, always winged, he is often armed with Sword, as in Euripides' Alcestis, who also describes him dressed in black.

The letter associated with him is the Theta, his initial in Greek, as well as the Theta nigrum symbol. As a psychopompa divinity, sometimes his figure is confused with that of Hermes, particularly in the most ancient period. He was often associated, besides his brothers, with other negative personifications such as Geras (Old Age), Oizys (Suffering), Apate (the Deception), Eris (Discordia). Occasionally it is seen as Death in peace, as opposed to his sister Ker, the Violent Death.

Oneiroi

Oneiroi are generated by Night, and consist in the dreams of mortals. They are the personification of it and they would be found on the shores of the west ocean, in a cavern bordering the domain of Hades, the god of the Underworld.

These gods send dreams to mortals through two gates or portals: one built with horns, the other in ivory.

From the first one real dreams take shape, from the second those deceivers. Each of them had its own role in shaping the dreams of mortals.

The three Oneiroi brothers are:

- Morpheus (Morpheus) - The most powerful of the Oneiroi, is "the modeller", the one who makes the dream take shape.
- It allows the manifestation of human beings within dreams. According to mythology, Morpheus brushed the eyelids of the dreamers with a bunch of poppies to take the shape of the dreamed person and was surrounded by imps that created the imagination.
- Fobetore (Phobetor, also called Icelo or Icelus) - "The scary"; he appears in dreams in the form of aberrant beings, such as beasts or monsters.
- Fantasas (Phantasos) - "The apparition"; all inanimate objects dreamed of by mortals are generated by him.

Fobos

It was the deification of fear and brother of Deimos, the terror caused by the war.
However, these evil personifications also had good brothers and sisters, like Armonia, the bride of Cadmus.
His major temple was in Sparta and the Spartans prayed in the temple before going down into battle. Plutarch reports, in the "Life of Alexander", that even Alexander the Great, on the eve of the battle of Gaugamela against the Persian king Darius, made sacrifices to this god.

Lissa

Lissa is the goddess of anger and blind rage.
It is frequently associated with Mania, another affine goddess of Roman mythology.
She was one of the nurses of Eros and is the daughter of Nix, who became pregnant with the blood drops of Uranus when he was emasculated. The most famous myth about Lissa is that he drove young Atteone's dogs crazy to kill their master, after the hunter had seen Artemis naked while taking a bath, and had not looked away. Lissa is represented by Euripides as a fury, with snakes in place of the hair, conducted by order of Hera from Iris in the presence of Heracles for taking possession of it; the hero, mad by blind rage, kills his wife and children. Represents a character quite ruthless and full of excellent facets, first of all the cruelty that, however, while representing the sheer madness of Heracles is characterized by a minimum of reason, as befits all demons: does not share the choice of Era and he rebels against his decision, but being forced to act, he does it, in the most terrible, ruthless and cruel way.

Alfeo

Alphaeus is in Greek mythology son of Oceano and Teti and personification of the largest river in the Peloponnese, which flows near the city of Olympia in Greece.
The nymph Arethusa, of which Alphaeus was in love, to escape his courtship, fled to Sicily and, near Syracuse, thanks to Artemis, became a source.
The god, in love, in order to return to her, begged Zeus to change the course of the river of which he was master.
Zeus, moved by Alfeo, allowed him to deviate his course, passing under the waters of the Ionian Sea to flow precisely near Syracuse, on the island of Ortigia where he would meet again the nymph Arethusa.
The deviation of the river Alpheus also occurs in the fifth of the twelve labors of Heracles, consisting in cleaning the stables of Augìa, which would have been overcome by diverting the waters of Alpheus who along their new path would have met and washed the stables and carried with them all the accumulated manure. It is also told of a legend according to which a cup thrown into the river Alpheus would then re-emerge in the Aretusa source. This legend refers to the main feature of the river Alpheus to flow almost entirely underground.

Acheloos

Acheloo, in Greek mythology, is the river god of Etolia, son of the Titano Oceano and his sister Teti. It is the second river, by length, of Greece and corresponds to today's Aspropotamo. According to the legend, Acheloo fell in love with Deianira, daughter of Eneo and Altea, and he contested his hand to Heracles. The fight began and Achelous, who had the faculty of assuming the appearance he liked best, turned into a huge snake that Heracles managed, almost, to suffocate. He became a bull, but he was defeated and thrown into the river. In the fall, one of the two horns that Heracles had seized, broke away, mutilating Acheloo forever. He considered himself defeated and gave him the right to marry Deianira, but requested his horn, giving him a horn of the goat Amalthea, the nurse of Zeus.

The nymphs Naiadi, filled the horn of Achelous with flowers and fruits consecrating it to the goddess of abundance and hence the legend of the cornucopia. From the drops of blood that fell from his wound the sirens were born, called, in fact, Acheloides from the name of the centaur father. According to another tradition, these would instead be born from the union of Acheloo with the muse Melpomene. He was also considered the father of many sources, such as the Pyrene source of Corinth, the Castalia source of Delphi and the Dirce source of Thebes. Even Calliroe, who married Alcmeone, is considered her daughter, but tradition does not mention her mother. It is also named as a protector of fresh water, so much so that Virgilio refers generally to waters like Acheloia pocula.

One of the interpretations that is given to this episode is that Acheloo was nothing more than a river of Etolia that reminded a snake because of its sinuous path, which frequently overflowed in an irrepressible manner as the charge of a bull. When Heracles arrived, he lowered his course, forcing him to run into a single bed (the allegory with the torn horn) thus bringing prosperity to the regions he passed through. From the earliest times it was held in great veneration for the proximity of the oracle of Dodona, which, with each response, added the obligation of sacrifice to the Achelous.

It was therefore invoked also in the sacrifices, in the prayers and in the oaths, and perhaps for this reason it was given its name also to other minor rivers of Thessaly and of the Arcadia. It was often depicted on vascular paintings, especially in Attic ceramics with black and red figures, in particular while fighting with Heracles. He often returns also in coin figurations.

Apeliote

Apeliote is a figure of Greek mythology, he was the son of Astreus and Eos, and brother of Borea, Euro, Calcias, Noto, Lips, Zephyrus and Sciron. Like his brothers, he was the personification of a wind, in particular, he was the god of the East wind.

He was considered a bearer of rain, beneficial for the crops, and was for this reason especially loved by the peasants. This is why he was portrayed as a young man with infantile features, with a flowing curly hair, dressed in green and holding fruit, wheat and flowers in his hand.

Asclepius

Asclepius, whom the Romans knew as Aesculapius, in ancient Greece was the god of medicine. Son of Apollo and Coronis, he was entrusted by his father to the centaur Chiron who taught him medical art. Having then dared to recall the dead to life, he was electrocuted by Zeus. The attributes of Asclepius were the stick, the scroll of a book, the bundle of poppies, but above all the snake; according to a legend a snake would bring him the miraculous grass that served to resuscitate Hippolytus son of Theseus, and after his death Asclepius and the serpent were placed in heaven, depicted in the constellation of Ophiuchus or Serpent and the Serpent. At the beginning, Asclepius was portrayed young and beardless, but then he came to represent him as a man in full force, his face surrounded by a thick beard and suffused with an expression of meekness and goodness.

The legend of Asclepius

It was at that time Coronis, daughter of Flegia, king of the Lapiths, the lover of the god Apollo. The legends narrate that one day the god, having turned away from Coronis, entrusted the custody of a raven by the snow-white feathers.
Coronis, who was attracted by Ischi son of Elato, took advantage of the absence of Apollo to receive Ischi in his bed.
The raven, who had witnessed the scene, immediately rushed to Apollo to warn him of what was happening and these, blinded by jealousy, killed Coronis and his lover by shooting two arrows from his bow: one for the unfaithful to the other for the his lover (according to another version it was Artemis who killed Coronis at the request of Apollo). Coronis on the verge of death revealed to Apollo that she was pregnant and that the baby would be born shortly thereafter. At that point Apollo, distraught by the pain of the gesture he had made, first cursed the raven who had warned him with such zeal but without telling him exactly how they were doing, condemning him and all his progeny to have the black feathers like the night. Secondly, he took his still alive son

from the womb and held him in his arms (according to other versions it was Ermes who took the newborn from the womb on the exhortation of Apollo).

The boy was called Asclepius and was entrusted by his father to the care and teachings of the wise centaur Chiron at the foot of Mount Pelo, where the centaur lived. King Flegia, the father of Coronis, learned of his daughter's death, blinded by anger, went with his army to Delphi and destroyed the temple dedicated to Apollo who, in order to take revenge for the outrage, flung one of his arrows at Flegia killing him. Meanwhile Asclepius grew strong and wise thanks to the teachings of Chiron and the more time passed and the more he became skilled and wise in the use of medicines and surgical instruments so much that he decided to make available to all the people who suffered from illness, his knowledge.

One day Asclepius received as a gift from Athena two vials: one containing the blood gushed from the veins of the left side of the body of Gorgona Medusa who had the power to resuscitate the dead; another with the blood that was leaking from the right side of the same body but that had the power to kill. Legend has it that Asclepius would have cured the Pretidae from madness, from the blindness of the Endides, from the wounds of Hercules.

But then his ambition grows: he wants to defeat the death that dominates life. The dead are raised: Orione, Capaneo, Glauco, Ippolito, Tindareo and others. Everything proceeded for the better until Hades, who reigned over the world of the deceased, went to Zeus to ask him to stop Asclepius because in his judgment he was subverting the natural order of things and the laws of nature itself.

Zeus, after having carefully listened to him, gave him reason and decided that the work of Asclepius should be interrupted and so he threw his lightning on him, killing him. Apollo, having learned his son's death and disapproving of Zeus's behavior, went to the home of the Cyclops, who had the task of creating the lightnings for Zeus, and killed them all. Asclepius after his death was rewarded by Zeus for his wisdom that elevated him to the rank of divinity, making him raise temples and statues.

Zeus made him a constellation, the constellation of Ophiucus (Ophiucus) from the Greek "ofiókos = he who holds the snake": we see it from the month of May and until September and is represented as a man holding in his hands a snake and for this reason it is also called Serpentario.

Snakes were consecrated to Asclepius. A legend tells, in fact, that one day while he was thinking about how to resurrect Glaucus (son of Minos and Pasifae) held a stick in his hand on which a snake tried to climb. Asclepius, annoyed, killed him with sticks. Shortly thereafter another snake arrived, resting a grass on the head of the dead snake and this resurrected. Then Asclepius took that same herb and brought Glaucus back to life. Hence probably the association of the snake with Asclepius. In Asclepius the science of medicine was consecrated and temples and statues were built up and quickly his cult spread throughout the known world, becoming the father of medicine. For the Romans the cult of Asclepius became the cult of Aesculapius introduced in 293 B.C by order of the Sibillini Books to stop a terrible epidemic.

The first place of worship of Asclepius was a cave near Tricca, where under the symbol of its main attribute, the serpent, gave oracles. Then the cult extended to Epidaurus, which was to become its main center, in Coo, in Athens and in the whole Hellenic world. The Asclepiee or Asclepiadee festivals were dedicated to him; to him the people of the Asclepiades, who all practiced medical art, including Hippocrates himself, the most famous doctor of antiquity, traced his origin. The shrines dedicated to Asclepius, the so-called Asclepiei, consisted of a source or a well, surrounded by a sacred wood, and the clinic, called adyton. We know little about the medical practice followed in those places, also because of the mysteries that surrounded it. The sick spent a night in the adyton; after a dream, probably obtained by artificial means, he followed the healing. However, it certainly was not the effect of the thaumaturgical power of the sacred place or merely the result of suggestion, but also of surgical interventions and propitious medicines.

From his wife Lampezia - according to others, from Epiona - Asclepius had six daughters and three sons:

- Igea - health and hygiene goddess. In Greek and Roman religion, the cult of Igea is closely associated with that of the father Asclepius, thus protecting the entire state of health of the individual. Igea is invoked to prevent illness and physical damage; Asclepius for the treatment of diseases and the restoration of lost health.

- Panacea - personification of universal and omnipotent healing, obtained through plants.

- Iaso - personification of healing. In fact, its name derives from the healing power or healer that the father possessed.

- Egle - was considered a mother of grace. It is said of her that one day, she joined the satyrs Croni and Mnasilio who had tied Silenus' hands with garlands of flowers, because, being asleep, they feared his reaction. As soon as he was awake, he saw the nymph, whom he had fallen in love with, and asked her to release him, with the promise of singing for the two satyrs, because he had promised to do so many times. How he did, loosened by laces, in the presence of Egle.

- Meditrina - the healer.

- Acheso - supervised the healing process.

- Telesphorus - god of convalescence. Often accompanied by his sister, Igea, was represented with the head covered by a cap or Phrygian cap. It is probably born around the year 100 in the area of Pergamon (a temple is dedicated to him in the Asklepieion of Pergamum), as part of the great cult of Asclepius present in the area. Its popularity has increased in the second century after Epidaurus: its representations are mainly found in Anatolia and in the regions near the Danube.

- Macaone - Famous doctor, he learned his healing arts from his father and master Chiron. He was among Elena's suitors. He arrived at the port of Aulis together with his brother Podalirius, bringing with him 40 ships. He treated the wounds of the Achaeans but still fought in battles. He healed Menelaus's wound caused by Pandaro's arrow. He was wounded when the Trojans attacked the Achaean wall and was forced to retreat together with Nestor in his tent. He treated Filottete's ulcer when he was taken away from the island of Lemnos where he had been confined. According to the most accredited tradition, also recovered in the Aeneid, he was among the warriors who hid in the wooden horse and died at the hands of Euripilo, son of Telefo, according to another tradition he died before the conquest of Troy and it was the rider Penthesilea to kill him. His body was brought back to Greece by Nestor.

- Podalirius - Bound by the oath of Tindaro he arrived at the port of Aulis together with his brother Macaone, carrying with him thirty ships, ready for the famous Trojan war. Arriving at Troy, he distinguished himself among the Achaean lines as a brilliant doctor. He freed the Greeks from a violent epidemic under the city walls. Together with his brother he treated the ulcer of Filottete, taken away from his isolation on the island of Lesbos. Macaone was considered a surgeon, Podalirius a general practitioner. He avenged his brother's death by killing the rider who had pierced him. According to the most accredited tradition it was Euripilo, son of Telefo, to kill Macaone, and the latter was then killed in turn by Neoptolemus. After the war Podalirius settled in Caria, because an oracle (supposedly the oracle of Delphi) had predicted to settle in a country where heaven falls to earth. In fact, the region has such high mountains that it seems to support the sky. Here, King Dameto welcomed him happy because he had a daughter sick with an illness that seemed incurable but the young man easily managed to heal her. Dameto, as a sign of gratitude, gave him his daughter, Sirna, in marriage, from whom he named the city he founded in the region, Sirno.

Boreas

In Greek mythology, Borea is the personification of the North Wind, son of the titan Astreus and of Eos, goddess of the dawn, and brother of Noto, Apeliote and Zephyrus. He is portrayed as a bearded winged man, with two faces and flowing hair.
Borea fell in love with Orizia, daughter of King Erechtheus and kidnapped her. She had Calaide and Zete, who participated in the expedition of the Argonauts in search of the Golden Fleece, and Cleopatra. To the sons of Borea, Calaide and Zete, as soon as they became adults, wings appeared and they were chosen by Jason to participate in the mission of the recovery of the Golden Fleece.
As soon as the Argonauts landed in Salmidesso, Jason met King Fineo, son of Agenore. He asked him for information on the golden fleece and he said he would answer if they had freed him from the harpies that had tormented him for some time. Immediately Calaide and Zete flew with weapons in hand and the hideous creatures ran away.
Later they were to free the children of Fineo, had from Cleopatra and imprisoned because of Idea.
With the wife of King Driante he generated Bute instead. In addition, in the Aeneid there is mention of three young Thracian warriors, companions of Aeneas in exile, who Virgil says precisely descendants of Boreas, without giving more precise information about this kinship: they are killed in the war against the Italics at the hands of Clauso.
In memory of the alleged help given by Borea in the Battle of Capo Artemisio to the Athenians to defeat the Persian fleet, the Boreasmi were established, parties in his honor.
In Roman mythology it is equivalent to Kite.

Ebe

It is the deity of youth, daughter of Zeus and Hera. His figure appears several times in the Homeric poems and is also mentioned by Hesiod. In Mount Olympus, Ebe was the enophora, the handmaid of the deities, who needed nectar and ambrosia. His successor was the young Trojan prince Ganymede. In the book V of the Iliad it is also the one who immerses Brother Ares in the water, after the battle with Diomedes. In the Odyssey is the bride of Heracles (although the authenticity of the piece is not certain). Euripides, however, cites it in the Heraclids. Myths related to Ebe have not survived.

In art, it is a famous statue of Antonio Canova, of which there are four versions: in addition to the one kept in Forlì, in the San Domenico Museum in a specially dedicated room, it is possible to admire a superb plaster version at the Modern Art Gallery of Milan. The corresponding goddess in Roman mythology is Iuventas, while its opposite in Greek mythology is Geras. It is mentioned in Theogony as a daughter of Zeus and of Hera as Ilia and Ares. Yet, a vivid tradition wants you to be only a daughter of Era - sitting down on a lettuce points out a late source. Olen makes Era the mother of Hebe and Ares, without mentioning his father; Pindar does the same for Ebe and Ilizia.

In the Iliad, where his ancestry is mentioned three times: he serves the cup-shaped Gods, pouring them ambrosia and nectar; he takes care of the wounds that Diomedes inflicted on his brother Ares; It helps Hera to hook up his wagon. The first role of cupping does not seem to be its main activity: it is mentioned only once, the Iliad also mentions Hephaestus to this office. Iris is more frequently associated with this role, both in texts and in iconography, before being replaced by Ganymede.

According to the Odyssey, the Theogony and the catalog of women, she married Heracles after the apotheosis of this. He has two sons Alessiare and Aniceto. Despite this, the theme of the ascent to Heaven of the hero, which can be dated from the 6th century BC, seems to suggest that these quotations are interpolated.

Aristarchus of Samothrace had already denied the incriminated passage of the Odyssey, considering it as contradictory with that of the Iliad in which Ebe takes a bath at Ares, saying that the fact of wetting someone is the duty of young girls - wrongly because the bath is prepared rather from domestic servants. Considering that eternal youth is one of the characteristics of the Olympian Gods it is difficult to evaluate exactly its role. Perhaps in an archaic period of the myth its presence was necessary to give the gods their perennial youth. A famous temple in Corinth was dedicated to Ebe and was particularly revered to Sycione, to Flio and to Athens where there was an altar dedicated to her, in the Athenian gymnasium of Cinosarge near that of Heracles.

In Greek art, Ebe is most often represented in the company of Heracles. A corinthian of Corinth and some Attic vase, with black or red figures, also depict his marriage with a hero on Olympus. It appears equally as a cup of Zeus or Hera on red-figured Attic vases, but without its identification being certain. Furthermore, she is often portrayed as a companion of the Goddess Aphrodite. It is often seen as a sweet young girl.

Aeolus

He is the god of winds. Born mortal, then became god.
Poseidon and Melanippe, the daughter of Aeolus, the ancestor of the Aeolians, had twins, Beolzio, and Aeolus. These were raised by a herdsman, that Hippie, since Poseidon did not want to let Eolo (Melanippe's father) know that he was his son-in-law.
Meanwhile Metaponto, king of Icaria, had threatened to repudiate his wife Teano, since it was sterile. Teano then got the twins to give Hippie, pretending they were his. Metaponto believed it. Only two twins were born in Teano, but they were the least loved by Metaponto. Teano, jealous, tried to kill Beoto and Aeolus with poison, which these, accortisi, gave to his half brothers.
Teano pierced his chest to see his little ones killed by the same breast that nursed them. Eolo and Beoto took refuge at first from Hippos, but then, when Metaponto learned from Poseidon how things had really gone, he married Melanippe and adopted the twins. After a happy period, Metaponto decided to repudiate Melanippe and marry that Autolyte, who the twins killed rotted with shame.
So they had to escape. Beozio returned to his grandfather Eolo, who entrusted him with the southern part of his kingdom, Boeotia, where the Beothis rose. Aeolus, on the other hand, escaped to the west, where he reached islands that he called Aeolian, where he became famous as an advisor to the gods and a tamer of winds. He lived in Lipari, a floating island, along with his twelve sons, six males and six females, who had married each other. When Zeus decided to lock up the winds in some amphorae, because he considered them dangerous if left in freedom, his wife Hera suggested hiding them in a cave in the Tyrrhenian Sea and entrusting their custody to Aeolus. At the time of his death Eolo, considered too precious by Zeus, remained guarding the winds in the cave of the Aeolian islands: he became so immortal. For Era Eolo he was like the other

Olympians, but Poseidon considered him an intruder, since he considered himself the master of the sea and the air.

Eolo is also mentioned in the Odyssey. When Ulysses, returning from the Trojan war, landed in the Aeolian Islands, Eolo hosted him and, moved by the story of the Greek hero, he gave him the skin of the skin in which the winds were opposed to navigation. During the journey Ulysses only blew the sweet Zephyr but while the hero was sleeping, the companions of navigation, believing that the oat regalatale from Aeolus was full of treasures, opened it freeing the winds that triggered a terrible storm from which it was saved only the ship of Ulysses. According to research, the sons of Aeolus were: Astioco, Xutho, Androcle, Feremone, Giocasto and Agatirno. Everyone, by the fame of their father and their virtues, reached a high consideration. It should be noted that Giocasto or Iocastro (Iokastos), was considered the mythical founder of the city of Reggio Calabria. Other traditions wanted the aforementioned city to be erected near his grave, where he had been buried after he died from the bite of a snake.

Fobos

Son of Ares, god of war, and Aphrodite, goddess of beauty, was the deification of fear and brother of Deimos, the terror caused by the war.

However, these evil personifications also had good brothers and sisters, like Armonia, the bride of Cadmus.

His major temple was in Sparta and the Spartans prayed in the temple before going down into battle.

Plutarch reports, in the "Life of Alexander", that even Alexander the Great, on the eve of the battle of Gaugamela against the Persian king Darius, made sacrifices to this god.

In ancient beliefs, the red blood awakens the god Fobos and, in fact, the maple (Maple pseudoplatano) was in the classical mythology the tree of the god of fear juxtaposition probably due to the blood red color of the leaves in autumn.

Iris

Iris or Iris is a goddess of Olympus, messenger of the gods and personification of the rainbow. She is the daughter of Titan Taumante and Oceanina Elettra, and sister of the three terrible harpies.
Unlike Hermes, the "fast" Iris does not belong to the Hellenic cult, but only to the myth. It is dressed in "iridescent" drops of dew and it is precisely because of its luminosity of variable color that the membrane of the eye is called "iris".
The specific task of the goddess Iris was to announce to men fatal messages, since it was Hermes the god who carried propitious messages from the gods.
Iris carries out her task as a messenger thanks to large golden wings with which she runs swiftly to carry the orders of Zeus.
Since the rainbow appears after the storm, Iris is considered a goddess of the storm, and has sisters like Procella and the Harpies; this explains how his messages are often painful. In Alceo we find the only testimony of the marriage of Iris with golden wings with one of the winds, Zephyrus, with golden crowns. From Hermes, also a fast messenger, of whom he is sometimes a companion, Iris distinguished himself in that he is also a sensible and expert god, and he knows how to conduct things to a good end, while Iride has no other function than bringing embassies.
Fidia depicted it on the eastern pediment of the Parthenon in the act of leaving to bring the news of Athena's prodigious birth to the world. The poets claimed that the rainbow was the trace of his feet when he descended from Olympus to the earth to bring a message. Sometimes, the celestial phenomenon of the rainbow is still called: Iride scarf.

Morfeo

Morpheus is the son of Ipno and of Night.
He possesses large and powerful wings that rapidly lead him from one side of the earth to the other. And 'the god of dreams, which provokes by touching a bunch of poppies on the eyelids of those who sleep.
It is often accompanied by a circle of elves that represent illusions.
Its name derives from a Greek word that means "form": in fact, it used to assume the form of human beings to show itself to the men asleep during their dreams.
The idea of a divinity of dreams, Morpheus, is generally attributed to Ovid, who gave a name to the three sons of Ipno (sleep): Morpheus, Phobetor (Fobetore) and Phantasos (Fantas).
Morpheus sent dreams populated by human forms. The other two, respectively, those with animals and those with inanimate objects. His messenger was the fast and winged Hermes, between his Lord and the wayfarers.

Narcissus

Narcissus is a character from Greek mythology, famous for its beauty. Son of the nymph Liriope and of the river god Cefiso (or according to another version of Selene and Endymion), in the myth it appears incredibly cruel, as it disdains every person who loves it.

Following a divine punishment he falls in love with his own image reflected in a mirror of water and dies falling into the river where he was mirrored. The Hellenic version of the myth appears as a sort of moral account in which the proud and insensitive Narcissus is punished by the gods for rejecting all his male pretenders and, in a certain sense, Eros himself. The story is therefore thought of as a story of warning to young people. Until recently the two sources for this version of the myth were a compendium of the works of Conone, a Greek contemporary of Ovid, preserved in the Bibliotheca of Fozio and a piece of Pausanias, lived about 150 years after Ovid. A very similar story was however discovered in 2004 among the papyrus of Ossirinco, which is believed to have been written down by Partenio. This version precedes that of Ovid for at least fifty years.

The Greek myth tells that Narcissus had many lovers, whom he constantly rejected until they were desisted. Only a young boy, Aminia, did not give up, so that Narcissus gave him a sword to kill himself.

Aminia, obeying the will of Narcissus, was transfixed in front of his house, having first invoked the gods to obtain a just revenge. Revenge was accomplished when Narcissus, contemplating in a source his beauty, remained enchanted by his reflection, falling madly in love with himself. Completing the symmetry of the story, seized by despair and overwhelmed by repentance, Narciso took the sword he had donated to Aminia and killed himself. From the earth on which his blood was shed, it is said that the homonymous flower appeared for the first time.

In the story told by Ovid, probably based on the version of Partenio, but modified in order to increase its pathos, Eco, a nymph of the mountains, fell in love with a vain young man named Narciso, son of Cefiso, a river divinity, and the nymph Liriope. Cefiso had surrounded Liriope with its waterways and, so trapped, had seduced the nymph who gave birth to a child of exceptional beauty. Concerned about the future of the child, Liriope consulted the prophet Tiresias who predicted that Narcissus would reach old age, "if he had never known himself." When Narcissus reached the age of sixteen, he was a young man of such beauty that every inhabitant of the city, a man or a woman, young or old, fell in love with him, but Narcissus, proudly, rejected them all.

One day, while he was hunting deer, the nymph Eco furtively followed the handsome young man in the woods, eager to speak to him, but unable to speak first because he was forced to repeat always the last words of what was said to her; in fact, she had been punished by Giunone because he had distracted her with long stories while the other nymphs, lovers of Jupiter, were hiding. Narcissus, when he heard footsteps, shouted: "Who is there?", Eco replied: "Who is there?" And so he continued, until Eco showed himself and ran to embrace the handsome young man.

Narcissus, however, immediately turned away from the nymph telling her to leave him alone. Eco, with a broken heart, spent the rest of his life in solitary valleys, moaning for his unrequited love, until only his voice remained. Nemesis, listening to these lamentations, decided to punish the cruel Narcissus. The boy, while he was in the woods, came across a deep pool and crouched down on it to drink. As soon as he saw his reflection for the first time in his life, he fell madly in love with the handsome boy he was staring at, without realizing that he was himself.

Only after a while did he realize that the reflected image belonged to him and, realizing that he could never have obtained that love, he let himself die dying unnecessarily; Thus the prophecy of Tiresias was fulfilled.

When the Naiads and the Dryads wanted to take his body to place it on the funeral pyre, in its place they found a flower which was given the name narcissus. It is said that Narcissus, when he crossed the Styx, the river of the dead, to enter the

Underworld, appeared on the limpid waters of the river, hoping to admire his reflection again.

Another version of the myth, narrated by Pausanias, tells that Narcissus had a twin sister whom he fell in love with.

The girl died young and Narcissus, to find relief from his pain, went to a spring to mirror himself to find in his features the face of his beloved sister, imagining to have it before his eyes.

Nike

Nike is a character from Greek mythology, personification of victory; is depicted as a woman with wings, made from which derive the appellations of Vittoria Alata and Goddess Alata della Vittoria. Nike is the daughter of the titan Pallante and the nymph Stige and sister of Cratos (Potenza), Bia (Forza) and Zelos (Ardore).

According to classical mythology, Stige brought his four sons from Zeus when he was gathering allies for the War against the Titans: Zeus named Nike leader of his divine chariot, a role in which he is often portrayed in classical Greek art and named all four sentinels of his throne. Nike is closely linked to the goddess Athena; in fact, the two often make a couple (they are united by a very strong bond), and is one of the most recurrent figures on the ancient Greek coins.

Their bond led to the formation of the divine figure of Athena Nike to whom the temple was dedicated in ionic order, built around 425 BC. on the west side of the acropolis, near the Propylaea.

Here a statue of archaic cult represented it without wings, in fact Pausanias, traveler and geographer of the second century AD, tells that the Athenians cut off their wings because the goddess and, therefore, the victory, never stray from their city .

The only known statuary of Athena Nike dates back to just before 430 BC in pario lychnite marble and is kept in the Collection of the Sorgente Group Foundation in Rome. The preserved portion of the statue measures 93 cm and had to be winged, as shown by the well visible recessed hole. Probably placed in ancient times on a high pillar in an attic sanctuary or in a pro-Athenian environment, it depicted the one who was following and protecting the Athenian army away from their homeland, witnessing the triumph of the city. Nike was depicted as a young woman with large eagle wings, with an olive crown on her head and a palm branch in her hand. Its most famous statues are the Nike of Samothrace and the Nike of Peonio.

The first is a remarkable marble work found on the island of Samothrace; it was the votive gift for the naval victory that Demetrius Poliorcete reported on Ptolemy of Egypt at Salamis of Cyprus in 306 a. C. The second, by the sculptor Peonio, was a votive gift dedicated by the Messenians and the Naupaziis after the battle of Sfacteria (425 BC). The Nike of Samothrace is a Greek sculpture that represents the goddess Athena Nike ("Athene who wears victory"). The statue is discovered, in pieces, on April 15, 1863, on the island of Samothrace, by Charles Champoiseau, vice-consul of France provisionally in Andrinople. The bust and the body allow Champoiseau to identify a representation of Nike, the victory, traditionally represented as a winged woman.

The pieces are sent to the Louvre museum. The statue is first dated around 190 BC, a time when the Rodiensi, in war against Antiochus III, reported a series of victories. In 1875, an Austrian archaeological mission once again searched the locality. The large blocks of gray marble, found in the vicinity, are identified as the bow of a ship that serves as the base for the statue, a representation on the tetradracma Demetrio Poliorcete coined following his victory over Ptolemy at Salamis of Cyprus, in 306 B.C. The statue is then considered according to this model, that is, with a trumpet in hand. However, Jean Charbonneaux's discovery in 1950 of a straight hand contradicted this theory; in fact, the hand is largely open and the fingers are extended. The surveys also allow us to show that the monument was obliquely placed in a rectangular exedra located at the end of a terrace at the side of a hill. The normal sight of the statue is therefore on the left three-quarters, as evidenced by the important disparity of completion between the two sides of the statue - that of the right side is very rudimentary.

On these bases, and by means of some models (straight wing, left center, back of the bust), a complete reconstitution is carried out at the Louvre in 1884. High m. 2,75, in Paros marble, is undoubtedly one of the most important and sensational works of all the Hellenistic plastic production. The statue is placed at the crucial point of the museum; it stands majestically on top of the staircase designed by Hector Lefuel, which connects the Galerie d'Apollon and the Salon Carré.

Pan

The god Pan was, in Greek mythology, a non-Olympic deity, half man and half goat. He was usually recognized as a son of the god Hermes and the nymph Driope.

The name Pan derives from the greek paein, that is "grazing", and, in fact, Pan was the shepherd god, the god of the countryside, of the woods and pastures. In some myths it is described as the oldest of the Olympians, if it is true that he had drunk with milk from Amaltea, bred the dogs of Artemis and taught the divination art to Apollo.

It was also notoriously associated with Fauno, a male version (later a son, brother or husband, depending on the myth) of Fauna, and as such was the spirit of all natural creatures, later linked also to the forest (of which the god was Silvanus), to the abyss, to the deep.

From its name derives the term panic fear, because the god was angry with those who disturbed by emitting terrifying screams, thus causing an uncontrolled fear, panic, in fact. Some stories tell us that Pan himself was seen escaping from the fear he provoked. But the most famous myth linked to this feature is titanomachia, during which Pan saves the Olympians by emitting a scream and making Delfine escape. Plutarch in his De defectu oraculorum tells how Pan was the only god to die. During the reign of Tiberius the news of his death was revealed to that Tamo (Thamus), a Phoenician merchant who on his ship bound for Italy heard shouting, from the banks of Paxos: "Tamo, when you arrive in Palodes announces to all that the great god Pan is dead! " Scholars are divided between historical and allegorical meaning. According to Robert Graves, for example, the cry was not Thamous, Pan ho megas tethneke, "Tamo, the great god Pan is dead", but Tammuz Panmegas tethneke, "The omnipresent Tammuz is dead", ie the Babylonian god of nature, thus indicating the end of an obscure era polytheistic, of which he had "panic fear", and the beginning of a new world under the light of Christ, who died under the empire of Tiberius (thus Eusebius of Caesarea in his Praeparatio Evangelical).

It is a powerful and wild god, outwardly it is depicted with goat's legs and horns, with shaggy legs and hooves, while the bust is human, the bearded face and the terrible expression. He wanders through the woods, often to chase the nymphs, while he plays and dances. It is very agile, fast in the race and unbeatable in the jump.

It is principally referred to as God the Lord of the fields and woods in the sundial hour, protecting the flocks and herds, the mountain peaks are sacred to him. Traditionally, he wears a nebris, a fawn skin. Legend has it that the nymph Driope fled terrified by the deformed appearance of the son, while the god Hermes picked it up and wrapped it lovingly in a hare skin, brought it on Olympus to entertain the gods, thus causing the laughter of Dionysus. Another myth is wanted by the son of Penelope and all his suitors, with whom he would have relationships waiting for her husband.

According to other sources he was the son of a lover between Zeus and the nymph Callistus from whom Pan and Arcade came to light. In another source it is believed to have been born of Zeus and Ybris, pure abstraction. Another version, supported by Igino, states that Zeus, after joining a goat named Beroe, gave her a son, the god Egipan, or the goat form of Pan.

One of his myth tells of his love for the nymph Eco from which born two daughters, Iambe and Iunce. Pan did not live on Olympus: he was a terrestrial god who loved the woods, meadows and mountains. He preferred to wander the mountains of Arcadia, where the flocks grazed and raised bees. Pan was a perpetually cheerful god, revered but also feared. Tied in a visceral way to the nature and pleasures of the flesh, Pan is the only god with a myth about his death.

The news was spread by Tamo, a navigator, and brought anguish and despair into the world. Pan took part in the Titanomachia, having a fundamental role had to escape faster than all in the victory of Zeus on Typhon. Typhon was a monster who was born of Gaia and Tartarus, who wanted revenge on the death of their children, the Giants. When he tried to conquer Mount Olympus, the Gods fled terrorized by this monster. They went to Egypt, where they took on animal forms to hide themselves better:

- Zeus became a ram
- Aphrodite fish
- Apollo crow
- Dionysus goat
- It was a white cow
- Artemis a cat
- Ares a boar
- Hermes an ibis
- Pan only turned his bottom into a fish and hid in a river.

Only Athena did not hide, and denigrating the other gods convinced her father Zeus to go into battle against the monster. Although the god was armed, the monster managed to get the better of him, and locked him in the cave where Gaea had raised him. With his spirals, Tifone had cut off his hands and feet, which he had entrusted to his sister Delfine, whose body ended with the tail of a snake. The god Pan frightened this creature with a tremendous scream, and Hermes took away the tendons of Zeus. Zeus regained his strength, and the tendons, launched himself on a chariot drawn by winged horses against Typhon, targeting him with lightning.

Zeus managed to kill the monster, and buried it under Mount Etna, which since then emits the fire caused by all the lightning used in battle, as told by the Pseudo-Apollodoro. To thank Pan, Zeus made sure that his appearance was visible in the sky. So he created Capricorn. As a god linked to the earth and to the fertility of the fields, it is linked to the Moon, and to the forces of the great Mother. Among the myths that accompany him one who sees him seducer of Selene, which he presented hiding the goat hair under a white fleece. The Goddess did not recognize him and consented to the union. But most likely this myth is confused with the sacred unions of Cernunnos with the great Celtic mother, also seen the outward appearance of the two male divinities. Pan is a generous and good-natured god, always ready to help those who ask for his help.

As with Cernunnos, there is a current of thought that says that this pagan god would later be taken back by the Christian Church to use his image as an iconographic of Satan. Legend has it that in the age of Oro Pan he arrived in Lazio, where he was hosted by the god Saturn. In Greece, the presence of the god is placed in Arcadia. In Italy there is a deity that has many similarities with the depiction of Pan, it is the god Silvanus. Pan is a god with a strong sexual connotation, he loved both women and men, and if he could not own the object of his passion, he abandoned himself to unbelief. Many mythological stories tell us about this god and his relationship with the Nymphs he was trying to possess.

So much so that these were saved only by transforming themselves, even if often they did not disdain the attentions of the god. Eco generated Iunge and Iambe with him, then fell in love with Narciso and tormented for him until he became only a voice.

Eufeme, nourished by the muses, had Croto, the inventor of the applauses. The myth brings us the name of others of these Nymphs: Pitis, Selene. Perhaps the most important is Siringa. One of Pan's most famous myths concerns the origins of his characteristic musical instrument. Siringa was a beautiful water nymph of Arcadia, daughter of the god of the Ladone rivers. One day, returning from the hunt, he met Pan.

To escape his harassment, the nymph escaped without listening to the compliments of the god. He chased her from Mount Lycée until she reached her sisters, who immediately transformed her into a reed. When the wind blew through the reeds, a plaintive melody was heard. The god, still infatuated, not being able to identify which barrel had turned Siringa, took some and cut seven pieces of length decreasing (some versions support nine) and joined them side by side. Thus he created the musical instrument that brought the name of his beloved Siringa. Since then, Pan was rarely seen without it. One day Pan wanted to challenge Apollo who played the lyre divinely, but it was a friendly race, Pan knew he could not compete with the sound of the lyric of the music god. King Mida chose to referee the race. This king Midas, son of Gordius, king of Phrygia, was very rich but like many rich, eager for riches. It is said that once, having treated well the companions of Dionysus, the god wanted to give him a gift leaving him to choose.

Midas asked that everything he touched would become gold; he was satisfied but the gift eventually became a punishment as everything he brought to his mouth, like food and wine, turned into gold. The king begged Dionysus to take back his gift, the god advised him to take a bath in the river Pàttolo, the king followed the council and was saved; From that day on, the waters of the river transport golden straws. Returning to the race between Pan and Apollo, the ignorant king Midas in music chose Pan as a winner and then Apollo punished him by turning his ears into donkey ears. The king tried to cover his hideous ears under a hat but his barber saw them to cut off his hair and Mida made him promise to keep quiet, on pain of death. This secret weighed too heavily on the barber who dug a hole in the ground to get rid of it one day and confided the terrible secret to the hole: "King Midas has donkey ears".

Then he covered the hole with the earth on which grew reeds and when the wind moved them, they repeated the words that the barber had confided to the earth, so they all knew of King Midas' ears. The cult of Pan would have entered Attica only after the battle of Marathon. It is said, in fact, that when Fedippide ran from Athens to Sparta to ask for help at the time of the battle of Marathon (490 BC), while crossing Mount Pertenio in Arcadia, he was called by name of the god and questioned why the Athenians did not worship him, despite having always been generous with them. So, after the victory of Marathon, from which the Persians fled in prey to "panic fear", in Athens he was erected an altar and in honor of Pan were held sacrifices and parties.

Tiche

In Greek mythology, Tiche is the personification of fortune.
Tiche was the tutelary deity who presided over the prosperity of cities and states. Its importance grew in the Hellenistic age, so much so that the cities had their specific iconic version of the goddess, who wore a crown depicting the city walls. In the Homeric "Hymn to Demeter" Tiche was considered one of the Oceanines, daughters of the titan Oceano and of the nereide Teti.

In other versions it is the daughter of Hermes and Aphrodite. In medieval art the goddess is portrayed with a cornucopia and the wheel of fortune. His counterpart in Roman mythology is the goddess Fortuna. Tiche decides the fate of mortals, like playing with a bouncing ball and symbolizing the insecurity of decisions.

No one should therefore praise his good fortune or neglect to thank the gods, otherwise this leads to the intervention of Nemesis ("compensatory justice" or "divine justice." In fact, originally the Greek goddess distributed joy or pain according to the right, and then with "nemesis" we mean an event, a negative situation that follows a particularly fortunate period as an act of compensating justice distributed by fate.The idea that underlies the term is that the world responds to a law of harmony, for which the good should be compensated Evil from the Homeric tradition, Tiche is mentioned instead by Hesiod, its importance grew in the Hellenistic age, so that the cities had their specific iconic version of the goddess, who wore a crown depicting the walls of the city itself.

In Antioch and in Alexandria in particular, she is venerated as a protective goddess of the city, whose cult is identified starting from the second half of the 5th century BC In Antioch, the sculptor Eutichide, realizes the famous "Tiche" of Antioch. Tiche appears on some coins from the pre-Christian era, especially from the Aegean region. In the Middle Ages it is represented with the horn of abundance, with a rudder ("it is she who leads the life of men") now sitting, now standing, most of the time it is blind.

Fortune was defined for the first time strictly by Aristotle. For the philosopher, luck is an accidental cause in things ("in those things that do not happen nor always") that occur by choice in view of an end. Fortune is a particular form of chance for Aristotle.

The philosopher Severino Boezio, in the "De Consolazione philosophiae" compares Fortuna to a wheel that makes the lives of men turn; in fact, sometimes they are in a favorable position, sometimes not because Fortune, philosophically, refers to chance, to that something against which the human will can do nothing.

Triton

Tritone is the son of Poseidon, the god of the sea and of the nereid Amphitrite. He was the brother of Rode and Bentesicima. Triton had a conch horn that calmed storms with its sound and announced the arrival of the sea god.

Very well known for the help he gave to Jason and the Argonauts in finding the route to follow. Triton was depicted with the upper half human and the lower one in the shape of a fish, all the skin was green. In the iconography with the name of Triton it is used a large number of minor marine deities that accompany Poseidon.

He generally passed by a prudent and benevolent deity who would welcome the Argonauts, driven by a storm on the shores of Libya where he lived. It was he who appeared under the characteristics of Euripilo, gave a clod of earth to Euphémos, as a gift and a sign of hospitality, and indicated to the navigators the road to follow to reach the Mediterranean. Triton also appears in a local legend, in Tanagra.

It is said that, during a festival of Dionysius, the women of the village bathed in the lake. While they were swimming, Triton followed them, scaring them. Dionisio intervened to help them and put Tritone on the run. It was said, too, that he would let himself go raiding along the edge of his lake, stealing flocks, etc., until the day a pitcher of wine was placed on the bank of the lake. Triton, attracted by the smell, approached, and drank. Then, drunk, he fell asleep on the spot, which allowed him to be killed. Thus the victory of Dionysius on the sea god was interpreted.

In the battle between the gods and the Giants, he also wore a trident like his father Poseidon. In a myth about the childhood of Athena it is said that Triton had a daughter, Pallas, with whom the goddess played and that, during an anger, the goddess accidentally killed. Tradition knows another daughter of Triton, a priestess of Athena called Triteia, who was loved by Ares, from whom she had a son, Melanippus, who founded the city of Triteia in Achaea, attributing her the name of her mother.

Zefiro

In Greek mythology, Zephyr was the personification of the west or northwest wind. Son of Astreus (or of Aeolus, god of winds) and of Eos (the aurora), he was often mentioned together with his brother Borea, the north wind and, like him, lived in a cave in Thrace. They attribute to him as kingdom "the places where the star of the evening rises, where the sun extinguishes its last fires (Ovid, Metamorphosis)." He joined with one of the Harpies, Celeno, who had assumed the appearance of a mare; the union of the famous and immortal horses Xanto and Balio that were offered to Achilles, as well as Flogeo and Arpago, the horses of the Dioscuri, according to some traditions, was also the father of Eros by Iris.

Chloris, goddess of flowers, from whom she had Carpo (the fruit), fell in love with the young Spartan prince Giacinto, and disputed him to Apollo, blinded by jealousy, he diverted the disk thrown by the god who struck Hyacinthus and killed him. other winds, sacrifices in his honor took place several times a year: the goal was to blow Zephyr or, on the contrary, to keep him distant according to agricultural needs.An Zephyr was called an altar in Athens.

Zephyr is a violent wind o rainy In the Odyssey and subsequent texts, it is considered, on the contrary, as a soft and light wind, a warm breeze that brings the announcement of spring. Zephyr is mentioned at the same time as Borea, and reprimanded by Poseidon (Neptune) for obeying the orders of Hera (Juno) and having started the storm that opened the Italian banks to Enea.

Like all winds, Zephyr is represented in Greek art as a winged character. Therefore, it is sometimes difficult to distinguish it from Eros. The depictions on the vases and on the amphorae generally show it together with Giacinto or in his arms. The scene presents an erotic character: on a vase of the Museum of Fine Arts in Boston, the sex in erection of the god fits into the folds of the young man's clothes.

Zephyr is also represented together with Chloris; the most famous representation of the couple is certainly that of Botticelli in the "Primavera" and the "Birth of Venus". Zephyr in Roman mythology is identified as Favonio.

The favonio (from the Latin favonius from favere, to grow), in German Föhn, is a wind that presents itself when a current is forced to overcome a mountain range. Both Favonio and Föhn derive from the Latin favonius, the name by which the Romans called the west wind.